The Blessed Life

The
BLESSED LIFE

Discourses on Spirituality

Swami Ramakrishnananda Puri

Mata Amritanandamayi Center, San Ramon
California, United States

The Blessed Life

Discourses on Spirituality
by
Swami Ramakrishnananda Puri

Published by:
    Mata Amritanandamayi Center
    P.O. Box 613
    San Ramon, CA 94583
    United States

In India:
    www.amritapuri.org
    inform@amritapuri.org

In Europe:
    www.amma-europe.org

In US:
    www.amma.org

Dedication

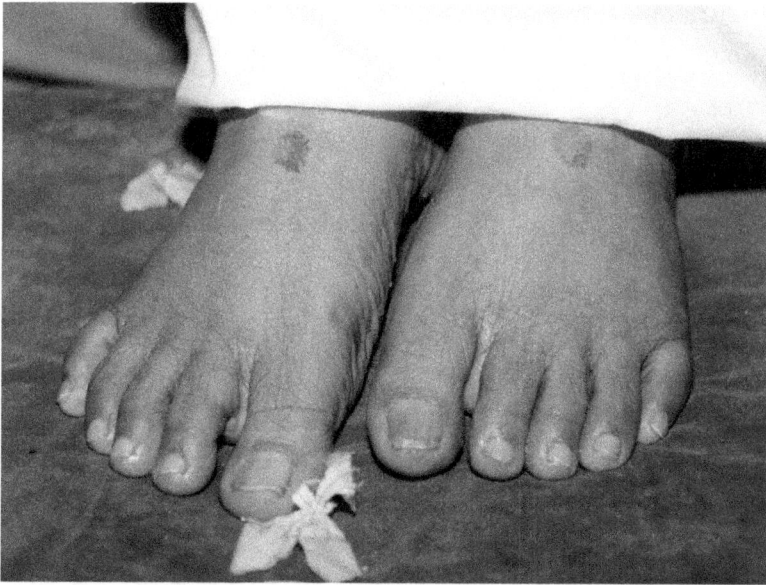

I humbly offer this book at the lotus feet of my beloved Satguru,
Sri Mata Amritanandamayi Devi

Durlabhaṁ trayam ev'aitat daiv'ānugraha-hetukam;
manuṣyatvaṁ mumukṣutvaṁ mahā-puruṣa-saṁśrayah.

*These three are difficult to obtain: to be born as a human,
to have the longing for release, and the association with
great souls. They are the results of divine grace.*

–Viveka Chudamani I.3

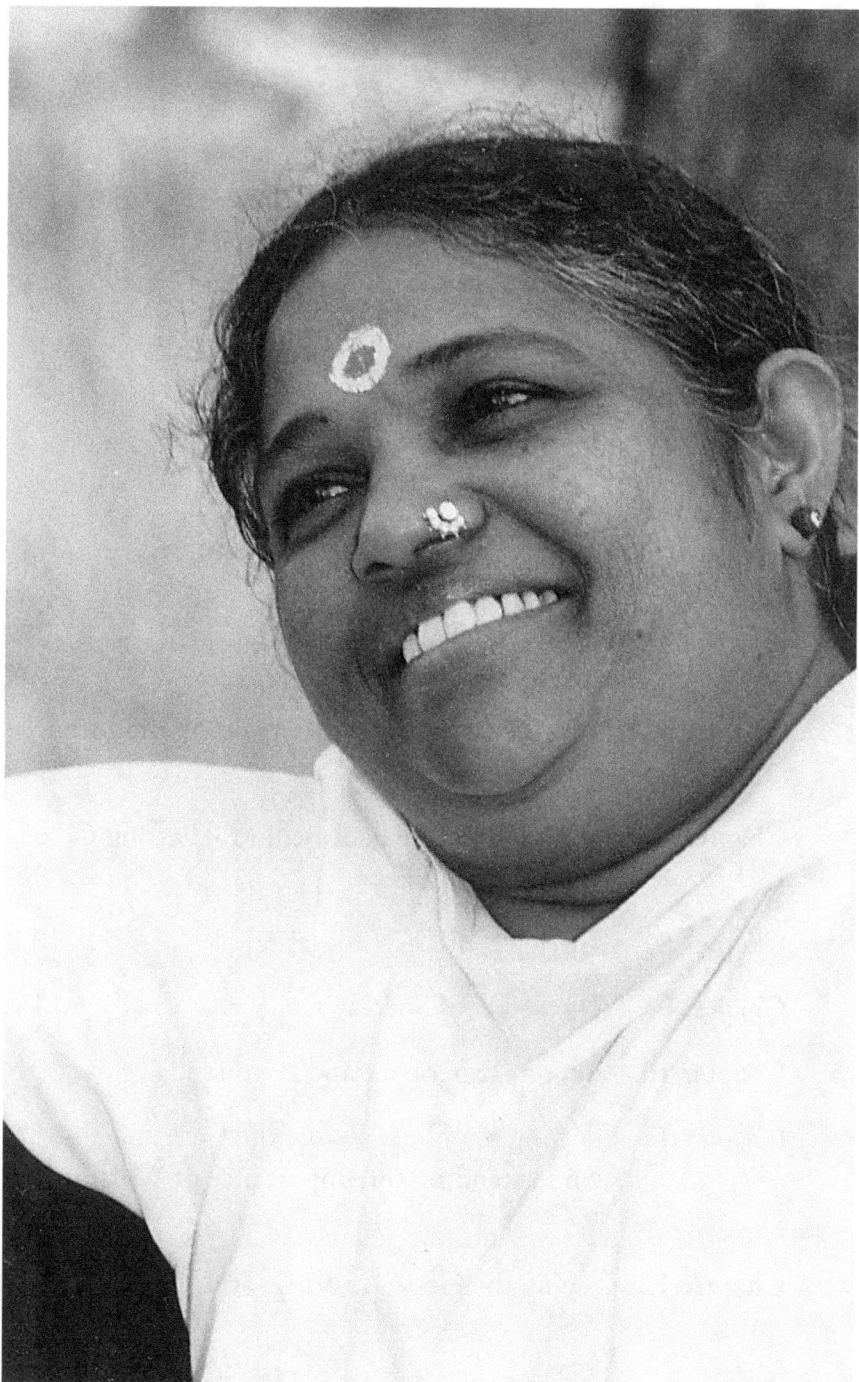

Contents

Introduction

At the age of 22, I was working in a bank in Southern Kerala and was not particularly interested in spirituality. I had grown up in a traditional Brahmin family but had never given religion or spirituality much thought. One day a client at the bank came in and started talking to me about a young holy woman known as "Amma" who lived in a fishing village not far away. One night after work, on a whim, I decided to go and see Her. I wanted to be transferred to a bank in my hometown, and I thought that if, indeed, She was a saint, Her blessing could help me reach my goal.

Amma was sitting inside a tiny temple. To my amazement, I saw that Her manner of blessing people was to give them each a hug, one by one. When my turn came, I did the same as everyone else: I knelt in front of Her and lay my head in Her lap. And then, as She embraced me, I spontaneously began to weep profusely. I had not cried since I was a schoolboy, yet in Amma's arms, my cheeks were streaked with tears. I had no idea what was happening to me. I thought, "There's nothing wrong in my life; I'm not sad at all; so why am I crying?" I felt as though my heart had completely opened—I felt totally vulnerable and yet, at the same time, utterly safe; I experienced a wonderful lightness of being. Though I had wanted to ask Amma for a blessing, I found that I could not say a word.

Something else happened that night that made an even deeper impression on me. The *darshan*[1] was coming to an end, and the last person was called in. A leper named Dattan entered the temple and went up to Amma. He had a particular kind of leprosy that made his body rupture in many places, with pus and blood oozing from the sores. A strong stench was emanating from his wounds. Almost everyone in the temple looked horrified and totally disgusted. People held their noses with the edges of their clothes. Some of them, afraid that Dattan's illness might be contagious, ran out of the temple. I was considering doing the same, but something made me stay. What I witnessed then was beyond anything I could have imagined.

Without showing the slightest hesitation and with an expression of glowing compassion on Her face, Amma made Dattan, who was kneeling in front of Her, place his head in Her lap, and She began to examine his wounds. To my astonishment, Amma then sucked the pus from some of the wounds and spat it out into a bowl. Other wounds She licked and added Her saliva.[2] Seeing this, my head began to spin, and I thought I would faint. A few others who were standing nearby closed their eyes, unable to take in the sight. Amma took almost 10 minutes to finish this task. She then applied some sacred ash on his body.

I thought, "Am I dreaming or is this really happening?" Here, I felt, was someone who surpassed even God in Her love and

---

[1] The word "darshan" literally means "to see." It is traditionally used in the context of meeting a holy person, seeing an image of God, or having a vision of God. In this book, darshan refers to Amma's motherly embrace, which is also a blessing.

[2] It is said that the saliva of a True Master has healing properties. In fact, within a few years, Dattan's sores closed over, and today he still visits the ashram—with some scars, but no longer suffering the dreaded disease.

compassion. A mother would hesitate to do such a thing for her own child, but here was one who did this to a leprous beggar!

I instinctively felt that the leper was safer with Amma than anywhere in the entire world. At that moment I decided that, come what may, I would always be with Amma; I would never leave Her.

The next time I went to see Amma, She told me to sit close to Her and meditate. I told Her that I had never meditated in my entire life. She just smiled and said, "No problem. Just sit here and close your eyes." I simply did what She told me to do. I closed my eyes and soon experienced a profound, ineffable peace. After what I thought was a few minutes, I opened my eyes and discovered that I had been sitting there for three hours! I thought something must be wrong with my watch and asked another person what the time was. It was true that three hours had passed. Even afterward, I felt a sense of deep joy and contentment.

The next day, I was still experiencing that wonderful sense of lightness. I went to the bank but couldn't concentrate on my work. I felt totally detached from everything. It took almost a week for me to feel like I was more or less back to my old self. And yet, I could not forget Amma and the inexplicable gift She had given me, simply by being who She was.

The third time I went to see Amma, She handed me a small picture of Madurai Meenakshi, the form of the Divine Mother installed in a famous temple in the city of Madurai, where I was born. I had always worshipped that particular goddess—but how did Amma know?

After these initial experiences, I would often wonder, "Who, exactly, is Amma?" Sometimes I would even directly ask Her. She never answered this question; She would simply smile. Then one day as I was meditating on the form of Meenakshi Devi, suddenly with my inner eye I saw Amma walking toward the form of the Goddess and merging into Her. I realized that this was the answer to my question—Amma was none other than the Divine Mother Herself. This is my firm faith.

Before meeting Amma, my greatest concerns were that the bed in the room I rented wasn't comfortable enough and that the food wasn't tasty enough. I kept longing for my mother's cooking and my own comfortable bed in my family home. Suddenly, staying with Amma, I found myself sleeping on the bare sand every night. What little food there was to eat was extremely plain. And yet, I felt completely fulfilled.

Amma showed me that what is really important in life is not bodily comforts or what fleeting happiness can be obtained in material pleasures and worldly relationships, but the realization of the *Atman*, the light of Consciousness that pervades, supports, and illuminates the entire universe, and is the True Self in all beings.

Those of us with some religious leanings may think of ourselves as having a soul, but we usually consider our soul to be a finite, separate being with almost as many limitations as our physical body. However, *Sanatana Dharma*[3] tells us that there is only one Soul, present in all beings. This Soul, or Self, can best be explained as the awareness, "I," without any conditions or circumstances attached to it. If we look deep within ourselves, ultimately we will discover that this "I" is the only permanence in a world of impermanence, that it is all-pervasive, and that to experience it in its pure state is to be absorbed in supreme, everlasting bliss.

One day, someone asked the Mullah Nasrudin, "Which is more valuable to humanity, the sun or the moon?"

---

[3] Sanatana Dharma is the original name for Hinduism. It means "The Eternal Way of Life."

"The moon, of course," the Mullah replied without missing a beat. "We need more light at night."

Just as the Mullah did not realize that the moon shines only by the light of the sun, we forget that everything in the universe derives its beauty and charm from the light of *Atman*. If we want to lead the blessed life that Amma is offering to us, we have to learn to put more of our focus on our True Self. This does not mean we can no longer enjoy what the world has to offer, but we can no longer completely ignore its Source, either. Amma gives the example of going on a picnic. Though we may be relaxing in the park, enjoying the sights, sounds and the delicious meal we have brought along with us, we never forget our home and the fact that we will have to return there soon. Like this, we should never forget our True Self, the *Atman*, and the fact that That alone will remain with us forever.

Amma's blessings are always there for us. Whether or not we receive them depends on our receptivity. If a bucket is turned upside down, it is not going to fill up even in a torrential downpour. A room will remain dark on the brightest of summer days if we don't bother to open the windows. Likewise, to become receptive, we may have to make some adjustments in the way we lead our lives. In this book we will try to explore the kinds of actions and attitudes that we can adopt in order to purify ourselves and allow Amma's grace to flow into us, making our life a truly blessed one.

Swami Ramakrishnananda Puri
Amritapuri, September 27 2005.

Amma's Life: In Her Own Words

"As long as there is enough strength in these hands to reach out to those who come to Her, to place Her hand on a crying person's shoulder, Amma will continue to do so... To lovingly caress people, to console and wipe their tears until the end of this mortal frame—this is Amma's wish."

– Amma

Born in a remote coastal village in Kerala, Southern India, Amma says that She always knew there was a higher reality beyond this changing world of names and forms. Even as a child, Amma expressed love and compassion to everyone. Amma says, "An unbroken stream of love flows from Amma to all beings in the universe. This is Amma's inborn nature."

About Her early years, Amma says, "Right from childhood, Amma wondered why people in the world have to suffer. Why must they be poor? Why must they starve? For example, in the area where Amma grew up, the people are fishermen. Some days they go out fishing but don't catch anything. And because of this, there are times when they have to go without food—sometimes for several days. Amma became very close with these villagers and had many chances to learn about the nature of the world by observing their lives and difficulties.

"Amma used to do all the household chores, one of which was feeding the many family cows and goats. To do so, every day She had to go to 30 or 40 houses in the neighborhood and collect tapioca peels and other such leftovers. Whenever She went to visit these houses, She always found that people were suffering—sometimes due to old age, sometimes poverty, sometimes disease. Amma would sit with them, listen to their problems, share their suffering and pray for them.

"Whenever She had time, Amma used to bring these people to Her parents' house. There, She would give them a hot bath and feed them, and occasionally She even took things from Her own house to give to these starving families.

"Amma observed that when children are young, they depend upon their parents, so they pray that their parents live for a long time and that they do not become sick. But when these same children grow up, they feel that their parents—who are now old—are a burden. They think, 'Why should I do all this work for my parents?' Feeding them, washing their clothes and treating them with care becomes a burden to these same children who previously prayed that their parents would live for a long time. Amma would always wonder, 'Why are there so many contradictions in this world? Why is there no real love? What is the real cause of all this suffering and what is the solution?'

"Even from early childhood, Amma knew that God—the Self, the Supreme Power—alone is Truth and that the world is not the absolute reality. Therefore She would spend long periods immersed in deep meditation. Amma's parents and relatives didn't understand what was happening. Out of ignorance, they began scolding Her and opposing Her spiritual practices."

But Amma was immersed in Her own world, totally unaffected by the criticism and chastisement of Her family. During this time, Amma had to spend days and nights outside, under the open sky, forgoing food and sleep. At that time, it was animals and birds that took care of Her, bringing Her food and stirring Her from deep meditative states.

Amma says, "During meditation and throughout the day, Amma would inquire into the source of all the sorrow and suffering She saw around Her. At one point She felt that the suffering of humanity was due to people's karma, the fruit of their past deeds. But Amma was not satisfied with this and went deeper. Then from within came the answer: 'If it is their karma to suffer, isn't it your dharma[1] to help them?' If somebody falls into a deep pit, is it correct to simply walk by, saying, 'Oh, it is their karma to suffer that way'? No, it is our duty to help them climb out.

"Experiencing Her oneness with all of creation, Amma realized that Her purpose in life was to uplift ailing humanity. It was then that Amma started this spiritual mission, spreading this message of Truth, love and compassion throughout the world by receiving one and all."

Today, Amma spends most of the year traveling throughout India and the world in order to uplift suffering humanity through Her words and the comfort of Her loving embrace. Her ashram is home to 3,000 people, and thousands more visit every day from all over India and the world. Ashram residents and visitors alike are inspired by Amma's example and dedicate themselves to serving the world. Through Am-ma's vast network of charitable projects, they build homes for the homeless, give pensions to the destitute, and provide medical care for the sick. Countless people all over the world are contributing to this loving endeavor. Most recently, Amma received international acclaim for dedicating more than $23 million for the relief and rehabilitation of tsunami victims in India, Sri Lanka and the Andaman & Nicobar Islands.

---

[1] In Sanskrit, dharma means "that which upholds (creation)." It is used to mean different things at different times, or more accurately, different aspects of the same thing. Here, the closest direct translation is "duty." Other meanings include: righteousness, harmony.

"In the end," Amma says, "love is the only medicine that can heal the wounds of the world. In this universe, it is love that binds everything together. As this awareness dawns within us, all disharmony will cease. Abiding peace alone will reign."

Part 1

Counting Our Blessings

"The human birth is precious. It is a gift from God."

– Amma

Chapter 1

The Blessing of a Human Life

Though God is present in all beings, in every object and the spaces in between, only we as human beings have the capacity to realize our innate oneness with this Supreme Consciousness that pervades all of creation. Attaining this realization, in fact, is the very purpose of life. If we do not make use of our life to put forth effort toward attaining this goal, we will find ourselves sinking ever deeper into the mire of attachment and its attendant suffering. If we are utterly careless in our thoughts, words and actions, we can even be reborn as a lower form of life.

It is said that before attaining a human life, a soul has to evolve through millions of lower life forms—from a blade of grass to a tree, from a worm to the bird that eats it, and so many other forms of life in all shapes and sizes. In the Buddhist tradition, there is the story of a bird clutching a silk ribbon in its beak. The bird flies over a mountaintop once a year, each time lightly brushing the peak of the mountain with the silk ribbon. The story goes that the amount of time it would take that bird and its ribbon to erode the mountain away into nothing is comparable to the amount of time it takes a soul to evolve to the state of a human being. From this we can understand how precious a human birth is.

Human life is a blessing, but if we do not make use of it in the right way, it can become a curse. We have all heard people say in a moment of despair, "I wish I were dead." But suppose we approach such a desperate person and offer a million dollars for his or her hands. They might agree to give up a kidney, but they will never give up their hands. Nor will they offer their legs, their eyes, their head, or their heart—the list goes on. Recently I read in a magazine that if we wanted to mechanically accomplish all of the functions performed by the human liver, it would take not one machine but an entire factory worth millions of dollars. Calculating in this way, we can see that God has made quite an investment on our behalf. Amma says that even a normal human body, let alone the attendant humane qualities, is invaluable. Unfortunately, most of us don't have the faintest idea how to make use of this precious gift of a human life. Before meeting Amma, I was in a similar condition; I had no idea what life was really for or how it was meant to be lived.

When we acquire a new appliance, inside the package we always find a user's manual with all the necessary information we need to know in order to use the item safely and efficiently—how to make the most of it.

Yet, there is one acquisition for which we have no user's manual. When we were born, we didn't get an owner's manual for our body, nor a user's guide for living peacefully and happily, for realizing the purpose of being born in this world.

If such a manual existed, wouldn't we want to see it? Wouldn't we want to go through it thoroughly every day? Actually, such a user's manual for a human birth does exist. The life and teachings of a *Satguru* (True Master) like Amma are the clearest and best guide to living our lives to their fullest potential, in the greatest harmony with the whole of creation.

The human being has not been created simply to live like any other animal, engaged in eating, sleeping, procreating and surviving. The purpose of the human birth and the human body is to ascend to the heights of Self-realization, or the knowledge that our true nature is none other than the Supreme Consciousness. Naturally, there will be difficulties and obstacles—the greater the goal, the greater the difficulty. For example, there are so many dangers and challenges involved in sending a rocket into space: the rocket has to break free of the earth's gravity; withstand the tremendous heat of the outer atmosphere and remain true to its intended orbit. If anything goes wrong, the human beings inside may lose their lives, but still, they risk everything for the goal. If the rocket remained on the ground, there wouldn't be any danger, but the very purpose of the rocket is to explore space, isn't it? What is the use of a rocket that never leaves the earth?

Similarly, if a human being simply lives like an animal, focusing on eating and sleeping, there is not much danger, but there is not likely to be any great achievement either. No one is going to force us onto the spiritual path; it is up to each of us to decide what to make of our life. But after reading the user's manual for a particular appliance, we typically find ourselves inspired to try to make it run as efficiently as possible. Likewise, when we sincerely study the life and teachings of the Masters, read the scriptures, and try to put the spiritual principles into practice in our own life, we will surely want to make the most of this rare and precious blessing of a human life.

Chapter 2

Knowing What We Don't Know

A man enters a room in a psychiatric hospital and sees two gentlemen sitting at a desk. Both are well-dressed, handsome and appear perfectly normal. Impressed by their appearance, the visitor approaches one of them and says, "Excuse me, sir, could you tell me why the other gentleman is here in this hospital? He seems so normal."

The first man replies, "Oh, he's completely bonkers. He thinks he's Jesus Christ."

Amused, the visitor asks the first man, "How do you know he isn't?"

The first man replies, "Because I'm God, and I don't even know him."

This answer sounds crazy, but what the man said is true: "I am God, and I don't even know him." In fact we are all God, but we are not aware of it. Even if we know it on an intellectual level, it is not part of our experience.

All of the Great Masters have tried to lead us to the realization of this same Truth. Christ said, "Love your neighbor as thy Self." Mohammed said, "If your enemy's donkey falls sick, care for it as your own." Amma puts it even more bluntly: "You are not different from me. I am you and you are me."

We may doubt the veracity of Amma's words, but there can be no doubt that, more than faith, this is Amma's personal experience.

If Amma did not feel our sorrow and pain as Her own, if She did not consider our problems as Her problems, would it be possible for Her to spend so much time—days upon months upon years—taking the world upon Her shoulder? We may have heard many times that Amma has given darshan to 24 million people in the last 30 years. But have we ever considered what that really means? When Dr. Jane Goodall presented Amma with the 2002 Gandhi-King Award for Non-violence, she described Amma as having given darshan to 21 million people. Then she paused and told the audience, "Think of it: *21 million people.*" The audience did think about it, and instantly erupted in thunderous applause. When we really step back and look at Amma's life as She has lived it, we can clearly see that Amma is the perfect example of the highest truth expounded in the scriptures—I am you and you are me.

Amma knows that teaching theory through words alone is not enough to bring about a change in the world. That is why She talks for 30-45 minutes, then gives darshan for anywhere from 6 to 24 hours. In this way She shows us how to see God in every being and in everything.

Without such an example before us, we tend to obey the dictates of our mind, which are motivated only by our selfish likes and dislikes. The shining example of the Sages of ancient times has always been available for us, and Amma is available for us, here and now. If we don't make the necessary effort to learn from Amma how to use this human birth properly and achieve the goal of life, there is no use blaming our manufacturer—God—for the problems we create.

The Greek philosopher Epictetus wrote, "It is impossible for anyone to begin to learn that which he thinks he already knows." In order to take advantage of the opportunity to learn from a True Master, we must be ready to admit that at present, we don't know anything about how to lead life intelligently, or at the very least, that there are things we don't know.

During one of Amma's recent European tours, a group of rough-looking youngsters entered the darshan hall. They were rowdy and noisy, and some people started complaining to the organizers about their disrespectful behavior. They seemed to be drunk, or even on drugs, and everyone became suspicious of them. After a while it came to the attention of the organizers that one of them had passed out. Immediately, everyone assumed it was due to intoxication or a drug overdose. After calling for an ambulance, they informed Amma of the situation, saying that it seemed he was drunk. Amma said to bring the youngster to Her immediately.

Amma took one look at him and then put a chocolate in his mouth, telling the others to make him lie down somewhere. The devotees were anxiously watching Her handling of the situation. I was also rather concerned. I told Amma, "Giving sweets to an intoxicated person will only worsen their intoxication."

As usual, Amma gave me some very good spiritual advice in return: "Keep quiet."

A few minutes later, the paramedics arrived and checked the boy thoroughly. Contrary to everyone's expectations, the boy's only problem was that his blood sugar was dangerously low. The paramedics said that Amma had done exactly the right thing: giving him a dose of sugar. The next time Amma came to that city, the young man brought many of his friends to see Amma.

The first time he came just for fun, but the second time he came truly seeking Amma's grace.

Of course, human nature is such that we always think we are in the right. We have so many preconceptions and false notions about ourselves and others and about what is best in life for us and for others. Even if they prove to be completely wrong, we feel very reluctant to let go of these preconceptions. This reminds me of a story I once heard about a man who ran into an old friend while walking down the street. He spied the person in front of him, and though he almost didn't recognize him, he was certain it was his old friend. Rushing up to meet him, he slapped him on the back, shouting, "Hey, Joe! How have you been, old pal? I haven't seen you in eons. I mean, I almost didn't even recognize you. You've gained about 30 pounds. You look like you've grown about two feet as well. And, I can see you've done some plastic surgery on your nose. You've even dyed your hair! I can't believe my eyes!"

The totally bewildered stranger replied, "I beg your pardon, but my name is not Joe."

Aghast, the first man replied, "My God! You've even changed your name!"

Similarly, no matter how obvious the evidence that comes before us, we always manage to mentally manipulate it and force it to fit our preconceptions so that we don't have to change our behavior or thought patterns. Even though Amma's words and guidance are the best ways for us to awaken and remove our ignorance, our mind will try to ignore the facts and find ways to justify its own ideas and opinions.

For example, Amma always tells us not to feel sad brooding over the past or become anxious worrying about the future. Hearing this, a college student once told Amma, "Since you told us not to worry about the future, I've decided not to study for my upcoming exams. Instead, I'm going to watch movies and go surfing." Obviously, this is a misinterpretation of Amma's teaching.

It is like the story of the doctor who decided to tell the truth to a man who was not long for this world. "If you want to know the facts, I don't think you have much time left. You are a very sick man. Now, is there anyone you would like to see?"

Bending down toward his patient, the doctor heard him feebly answer, "Yes."

"Who is it?" the doctor asked.

In a slightly stronger tone, the dying man said, "Another doctor."

This is the story of our relationship with Amma. Fortunately, Amma gives us endless opportunities to learn and helps us change our way of thinking. She has even said that She is ready to take any number of births for the sake of Her children. Through Her teachings and the example of Her life, Amma removes our preconceived ideas about the nature of reality, replacing them with a clear view of the nature of the world and our True Self. From this understanding, peace, love and positive virtues like patience, kindness and compassion naturally blossom within us.

Chapter 3

Changing World, Changeless Self

One day the Hebrew King Solomon decided to humble his most trusted minister. He said to him, "Benaiah, there is a certain ring that I want you to bring to me within six months."

"If it exists anywhere on earth, your majesty," replied Benaiah confidently, "I will find it and bring it to you. But what makes the ring so special?"

"It has magic powers," answered the king with a straight face. "If a happy man looks at it, he becomes sad, and if a sad man looks at it, he becomes happy." Solomon knew that no such ring existed in the world. Wishing to give his minister a little taste of humility, he was sending him on an impossible mission.

Spring and then summer passed by, and though he had searched the length and breadth of the kingdom, still Benaiah had no idea where he could find the ring. The night before the six months were up and he knew he would have to return to the king in defeat, he decided to take a walk in one of the poorest sections of Jerusalem. He passed by an old merchant who had begun to set out the day's wares on a shabby carpet. With nothing left to lose, Benaiah asked, "Have you by any chance heard of a magic ring that makes the happy wearer forget his joy and the broken-hearted wearer forget his sorrow?"

The old merchant did not speak, but took a plain gold ring from his carpet and engraved something on it. When Benaiah read the words on the ring, his face broke out in a wide grin.

That night Benaiah went to see the king as he was in court with all his ministers. "Well, my friend," Solomon smirked, "Have you brought me what I sent you for?" All the ministers chortled heartily, eager to see their peer admit his embarrassing defeat.

To everyone's surprise, Benaiah held up the small gold ring and declared, "Here it is, your majesty!" As soon as Solomon read the inscription, the smile vanished from his face. Into the ring, the jeweler had engraved the phrase, "This too shall pass." At that moment, Solomon realized that all his wealth, power and influence were fleeting indeed, and that he could not escape the fact that he, too, would one day be nothing but dust.

In the *Dhammapada*, the Buddha says,

> *Not in the sky,*
> *Nor in the midst of the ocean,*
> *Nor deep in the mountains,*
> *Nowhere*
> *Can you hide from your own death.*

Amma tells us to always remember that everything we find in the world around us, our bodies included, is changing and impermanent. However, this awareness is not meant to sink us into despair. Taken along with the knowledge that our True Self is changeless, eternal and of the nature of supreme bliss, this awareness can help us to get our priorities in order and inspire us to pursue the supreme dharma of Self-realization. Amma says that we always give first place to our body and last place to God, or our Self, when in fact we should give first place to the Self. If we can learn to place the appropriate value on our body and the other objects of the world—and the appropriate value on our Atman—we can use the impermanent body as a vehicle to realize the Permanent Atman. Even though the shadow cast by a tree is fundamentally impermanent, it is useful—we can stand there to get respite from the hot sun. Likewise, though the body and all the objects of the world are impermanent, each one has its practical uses. The problem arises only when we place too much importance on these objects, or expect to derive something from them that they are not capable of giving us.

In the history of India we find a great and powerful king named Bhartrihari. Like King Solomon, Bhartrihari learned a hard lesson in impermanence. After being throned as King, Bhartihari became so attached to his wife, the Queen Pingala, that he spent most of his time with her even at the expense of his kingly duties. When one of his advisors tried to talk some sense into him, Bhartrihari exiled the advisor from the city.

One day, a visiting hermit offered the king a special fruit. The hermit told the king that eating this special fruit would grant eternal youth. Due to his obsessive attachment toward Pingala, the king did not eat the fruit himself but gave it to the queen, for he could not bear the thought of her youthful beauty fading away with the passage of time.

The queen took the fruit from the king and promised to eat it after having her bath. What the king didn't know was that Pingala was in love with one of the palace stable-keepers. That night, she smuggled the fruit out of the palace and gave it to him. Meanwhile, unbeknownst to the queen, the stable-keeper's heart belonged to a local prostitute, and he, too, did not eat the fruit for himself but presented it to his beloved. Despite her livelihood, the prostitute had a sense of dharma, and decided that the fruit would be wasted on anyone but the king.

So it was that the day after the king had given this blessed fruit to his wife, the prostitute entered the court of the king as he was meeting with his council, and hesitantly presented it to the king, explaining its power as she did so.

Seeing the same fruit in the prostitute's hand, the king was confused. He demanded that the prostitute tell him where she had gotten it. She admitted that it had been given to her by the palace stable-keeper. Immediately, the king called the stable-keeper to his court. Believing that his life would be spared only for the sake of his honesty, the stable-keeper confessed that he had received it from none other than the queen.

The news was a great shock for King Bhartrihari. At the same time, it was a blessing—he was now able to overcome his unreasonable attachment toward his wife and realize that all worldly love has its limitations. In fact the king became so detached from the promise of happiness in the objects of the world that he renounced the entire kingdom with all its power and pleasure, and retired to the forest in search of everlasting peace in the knowledge of the Self.

This does not mean that we need to wait for a major shock in our lives in order to realize the impermanence of all that we call our own. We can easily gain this conviction by listening to the words of the scriptures and the True Masters. If that is not enough, there is plenty of evidence available in the world around us.

After the devastating tsunami of December 2004, Amma commented that the tsunami was a warning, but no one heard it. She challenged the ashramites and others to reflect on what could be learned from the tsunami.

"Unexpected situations like this teach us that nothing is really ours," Amma said at the time. "We cling on to things and people, thinking of them as our own, but such situations reveal that nothing is ours; our very life is not ours to hold on to.

"When we see an accident on the road, right in front of our eyes, it serves to make us more alert. Such situations help generate an awareness within. This awareness shows us the way—how to go forward.

"We hold on to the idea of 'me' and 'mine.' Everybody says *I* have done this, *I* have done that, but where does this 'I' come from? We see the sun only by the light of the sun. What we call our own is not really ours—what He gives, He takes away too. He gives, and we accept. And when He wishes, He takes back... it is with this attitude that we should accept situations in life."

Amma's words recalled the inspiring reaction of the villagers in Gujarat after the devastating 2001 earthquake razed their entire villages. Most of the households had lost one or more family members as well as the roof over their heads. When Amma visited them there and asked how they were faring, they answered with surprising equanimity and poise. "We are fine," they told Amma. "What God gave, He took away."

While enjoying the objects of the world, we do experience temporary happiness. Instead of allowing this momentary enjoyment to increase our faith in the world, we should remember that our life is like a pendulum, and when we are experiencing happiness, the pendulum is merely gaining momentum to swing toward sorrow. Amma says that true peace and contentment can only be found when the pendulum becomes still, in the center. This is not just an arbitrary law; it is the logical outcome of relying on external conditions to give us happiness. When the conditions change, we will experience sorrow. Even if the conditions do not change, the happiness is not going to remain. For instance, we might be really enjoying a particular movie. But suppose someone told us that movie was going to go on forever and we would not be able to leave the theater. Our happiness would disappear in a moment. Similarly, we may love to eat ice cream. But how much ice cream can we eat before we feel sick? There will come a point when we cannot stand to take another spoonful. This shows that happiness is not inherent in these objects and experiences—that even the pale happiness we can get from the world is fleeting. The only way to find true happiness is to look within and find the changeless Self.

Ordinary people experience happiness only through a particular medium—typically through sensory pleasure of some kind, through hearing words of praise, or through achieving a particular goal. *Mahatmas*[1], on the other hand, are capable of experiencing happiness without any medium. When Amma was forced to live out in the open, enduring blistering sun and pouring rain as well as abuse and even attempts on Her life, She would sit immersed in meditation for hours on end. What would be our condition if we were in a similar situation? We would not rest until we found a nice hotel or at least a friend with whom to stay. Our next concern would be something to eat, preferably with a friend to whom we could pour out our sorrows and talk about all the injustices done to us. And yet, Amma was not at all troubled by these conditions. Though She had no food, shelter or anyone to

---

[1] Mahatma literally means, "Great Soul." Though the term is now used more broadly, in this book Mahatma refers to one who abides in the Knowledge that he or she is one with the Universal Self, or Atman. All Satgurus, or True Masters, are Mahatmas, but not all Mahatmas are Satgurus. In many cases, the Mahatma does not show any interest in uplifting others, preferring to spend all his or her time absorbed in the bliss of the Self. The Satguru is one who, while still experiencing the bliss of the Self, chooses to come down to the level of ordinary people in order to help them grow spiritually.

call as a friend, She was perfectly content. Amma does not need any external medium to experience contentment, and yet, Her contentment is so much deeper than ours.

Whether we are aware of it or not, we are always having faith in someone or something's ability to bring us happiness. We are taking refuge in something, hoping that it will lead us closer to happiness. If it is not one thing, it's another. Amma says that our "refuge" is simply that to which our mind is constantly drawn and our thoughts flow—that in which our mind constantly abides. Keeping that definition in mind, it's not difficult to find out what we are taking refuge in now: our possessions, our job, our friends, recreation, and our emotions. Aren't these the things that we think about all the time?

Before discovering that tungsten was an effective filament for use in light bulbs, the story goes that Thomas Edison conducted more than 2000 experiments using materials that failed to conduct electricity and produce light. Many other scientists ridiculed his efforts, saying, "Even after conducting 2000 experiments, you haven't been able to prove anything."

Edison replied, "Not at all—I have proven that these 2000 materials won't work!"

Similarly, we need not feel bad about searching for happiness in worldly objects as long as we learn the right lesson. At the same time, just as the scientists following in Edison's footsteps need not conduct those same 2000 experiments, if we are ready to follow in the footsteps of the Great Masters, we do not need to go on searching for happiness outside ourselves.

It is worth mentioning that while the objects of the world have a limited capacity to make us happy, these same objects are unlimited in their capacity to bring us suffering. Those who look for happiness in cigarettes eventually get lung cancer and, after a protracted illness, die an early death. Those whose happiness lies in their beloved might even commit suicide when that person leaves them for someone else. Everyone wants to live in a big house—the bigger the better—but the bigger the house, the more repairs and maintenance will have to be done.

In the *Tao Te Ching*, Lao Tzu says,

> *Chase after money and security*
> *and your heart will never unclench.*
> *Care about people's approval*
> *and you will be their prisoner.*

Even before becoming the Buddha (the Awakened One), the young prince Siddartha may have had a clearer view on the nature of worldly happiness. Perhaps that is why he named his son "Rahula," meaning "fetter," or "bondage." This may sound harsh, but let us think about our own experience. We may find a new baby to be the source of inextinguishable happiness, but what about when the child reaches the "terrible two's"? Later on, when the child is a teenager, he or she may fall into bad company, become a bully or even hate his or her parents. There are many cases of children who even disown their parents as soon as they come of age. In such cases, what we thought would be a source of endless happiness becomes a source of endless sorrow.

This doesn't mean that we should not have children or seek happiness in the outside world, but we should expect unhappiness as well as happiness, and prepare ourselves to accept both with an equal mind. We should always remember not to expect too much from anything or anyone, and that God alone will remain with us forever. In other words, it is all right to enjoy the fleeting objects of the world around us, but we shouldn't take refuge in them. Instead, we should learn to take refuge in—to let our thoughts flow toward—God or Guru. Doesn't it make sense to take refuge only in something that will never leave us?

Just as a snake handler knows that it is the snake's nature to bite, we have to accept the fact that it is the nature of people to change their minds, attitudes and opinions. We should never expect that a person, object or situation will remain the same. Living with this understanding and acting accordingly is intelligent living. Amma gives the example of shifting the gears in a car. When we are driving up a steep hill, if we do not shift into a lower gear, we will not be able to move forward. And when driving fast, if we do not shift into a higher gear, we will destroy the engine. Likewise, when facing different situations in life, we must be able to properly adjust our mind to accept whatever comes with an attitude of equanimity.

No one wants to experience sorrow, even briefly. But we are not satisfied with the mere removal of sorrow; we also want to experience lasting happiness. Once a young man came to me and said, "I don't have any problems or sorrow, but I still don't feel content. Something is missing from my life. I have tried many things so far, but not spirituality. That is why I came here." This young man did not have any problems to solve, but still, he did not feel complete. He believed, correctly, that spirituality might hold the key to filling the inexplicable void in his life.

Lasting happiness cannot be obtained from something that doesn't last. The situations and objects of the world are constantly changing, and our awareness is usually focused on and identified with these changing circumstances. As a result, whenever the circumstances change, we are affected.

This is similar to what happens when we watch a movie. The various incidents in the movie affect us emotionally, even physiologically. In the villages of Tamil Nadu, there are movie stars who are so popular that the moviegoers become totally identified with their characters. Even if the hero gets a small scratch in a fight scene, everyone throws bottles and stones at the movie screen. If he or she starts crying during an emotional scene, we can hear many sobbing voices in the theater.

The audience gets so involved in the story that they are willing to totally suspend disbelief for the sake of being swept up in the drama, even though the events portrayed might be totally unrealistic. I heard about a recent movie with an action sequence wherein the hero and the villain are exchanging gunfire until the hero runs out of bullets. Sensing his sudden advantage, the villain takes aim and shoots a volley of bullets, hitting the hero in the thigh. For a moment, the audience is horror-stricken. They even think of burning down the movie theater. But the next moment, the hero pulls out the bullet that was lodged in his thigh, loads it into his own gun, and shoots and kills the villain. The theater erupts with thunderous applause; no one is at all bothered by the absurdity of the scene.

Amidst all this commotion, there is one thing that is totally involved in the movie but, at the same time, is not at all affected. It is the movie screen. Without the screen, the movie cannot be shown. But it remains totally unaffected; it is the changeless substratum for all the changing scenes.

Similarly, there is a changeless substratum for all the experiences we undergo in life. That is the Atman, or Self. This Self manifests as the awareness that allows us to perceive both the world outside, as well as our own body, thoughts, emotions, desires and attachments. In truth, it is not these changing mental formations but the changeless awareness behind them that is who we really are.

Instead of identifying with this changeless Self, we always identify with the different experiences, and thus our life becomes like an emotional roller coaster. Because of this, many of us suffer from a kind of identity crisis. Not the identity crisis we usually think of, related to our profession, personality or relationships—it runs much deeper than any of these. In this sense, even if we don't have the visible symptoms of an identity crisis, in fact we are all suffering from varying degrees of confusion about our identity.

The more we identify with our True Self, the less we suffer. The Mahatmas never suffer from any kind of identity crisis. In the strictest sense, only a Self-realized person can claim to know their true identity. As Amma says, "There was never a time when Amma did not know who She is."

When Amma was just a young woman, some of the villagers, who were resentful of Amma's strange, unorthodox behavior and jealous of Her growing popularity, threatened to kill Her, even brandishing a knife in front of Her. Amma was totally unaffected by their threats. She stood in front of them and boldly declared, "You can kill this body, but you cannot touch the Self."

Even today, Amma's attitude toward such situations remains unchanged. In August of 2005, when a stranger approached Amma with a concealed knife, apparently with the intent of putting an end to Her life, Amma was totally unperturbed. She did not even get up from the stage but continued to sing bhajans (devotional songs) and later gave the Devi Bhava Darshan[2] as previously scheduled. Though the ashramites and devotees all over the world were very disturbed by the incident, Amma took the

---

[2] Amma regularly gives a special darshan where She appears in the mood and dress of the Divine Mother. At that time, She is completely identified with God in the form of the Divine Mother. Earlier, She used to give darshan in Krishna Bhava as well.

whole situation in stride. Later that day, She answered questions from a group of reporters who came to the ashram immediately after the thwarted attack. Amma told the reporters with a carefree smile, "I don't have any reaction to this incident. I am not at all afraid of death… whatever is meant to happen will happen when the time comes. I just want to do what I have to do. Anyway, one day we all have to die. Therefore, it is better to get worn out working for others than to rust away."

Even amidst countless worldly responsibilities, Amma always maintains a spiritual outlook. In contrast, even while doing spiritual practices, our focus remains at the worldly level.

Amma says that the whole purpose of spirituality is to bring about a shift in our perception: from the worldly to the spiritual, from the external to the internal. Because of our inability to shift our perception, we waste a great deal of time and energy in trying to resolve our problems.

It is due to our lack of mental expansiveness that we are unable to face life's circumstances. As Amma often says, there are three ways in which we usually deal with the unpleasant circumstances in life: run away; tolerate but complain, or try to change the circumstances. No one tries to change what Amma calls their *manasthiti* (mental stance) in order to face the challenges in life. It is this process of changing our mental stance, not our external circumstances, that gives expansiveness of mind. At present, the extroversion of society and culture lead people to find the cause of suffering only in external circumstances. We rarely try to learn how to turn our attention inward, expand the mind, and resolve the problems that way.

It is true that the solution to some problems, like hunger or the need for shelter, can be found outside ourselves. But even then, sometimes an external solution will not be available. In the early days of the ashram, there were many times when there was not much left for Amma and the *brahmacharis* (celibate disciples) to eat after all the devotees had been served. And yet, there was so much tiresome physical work to do and nobody else to do it. Somehow, due to the inspiration we drew from Amma, we were able to summon up the stamina to do spiritual practices alongside physical work, even on a meager diet.

Everything depends on our conditioning. Amma says that spirituality is conditioning the mind to adapt to any circumstance and to find happiness within, independent of what's going on around us. In fact, for most of the problems in our life, the solutions can only come from within. Take, for example, the problems of anger, hatred, disappointment or jealousy. There are no external solutions to these problems; we have to find the solution within. If we seek external solutions to these problems, it can even lead to more problems in the future.

Recently a Westerner came to live at Amritapuri. In the West he had lived alone for many years, but when he came to the ashram, he had to share a room with another person. It was then that he discovered that he was very sensitive to noise. His roommate worked on a laptop computer in the room, and the newcomer discovered that the clicking of the roommate's electronic mouse really disturbed him while he was trying to meditate. He did not want to ask his roommate to curtail his work, so he decided to buy a special silent mouse for his roommate. After that he thought he would be able to meditate and study in peace, but now that the clicking of the mouse was gone he suddenly became aware of the rattling sound of the fan rotating in the room one floor beneath him. After weeks of restless meditation and tossing and turning at night, he finally decided to buy a silent fan for his downstairs neighbors. By then he was really sure that there would be no more disturbances for him. But with the rattling sound of the fan eliminated, he became aware that due to the tsunami relief work going on in the surrounding area, there were a lot of trucks passing by on the road beside the ashram. The roaring of the truck engines greatly disturbed him, but he knew it would not be possible to buy a whole fleet of silent trucks. It was then that he realized that he had been trying to solve an internal problem with external solutions, and what he really needed to do was to try to reduce his own internal sensitivity to noise.

Many of us pray to Amma to solve our problems, and of course Amma is happy to do so through Her divine resolve. But for each problem we will have to get a separate solution. The best type of help we can receive is one solution that works for many of our problems. This broad solution is the shift in perception that Amma is working to bring about in us. How can a simple shift in perception make such a difference?

Imagine there are two waves. One is an ignorant wave, and the other is a wise wave. The ignorant wave considers itself as nothing more than a wave, thinking, "I am a wave of a particular size, I came from another wave at such and such a time, and I will perish in the near future."

The wise wave will think differently: "I am not a wave at all. 'Wave' is just a name given to me. I am essentially water, and as water I was never born as a wave. I was always water, I am water now, and I will always be water. Even though this particular wave disappears, I will still exist as water."

An ignorant wave looks upon itself as a mortal wave, while a wise wave looks upon itself as the immortal water.

The moment the ignorant wave looks upon itself as a wave, it will see all sorts of differences in the other waves. It will see other waves as different from itself, as potential competitors—big or small, peaceful or violent—and this will create competition, jealousy, greed and other negative feelings.

The wise wave looks upon itself as water and other waves as also water. It sees everything as water alone—it sees no difference between itself and the other waves, or between itself and the ocean.

In the same way, a wise person will see everyone and everything as nothing but his or her own Self, whereas an ignorant person will see everyone and everything as separate and different from him or her. Even in a wise person, the physical eyes will see the differences between forms, but through the spiritual eye of wisdom, such a person will see everything as the same Atman.

Once, soon after I started staying at the ashram, I had gone on ashram business to Bangalore, and on the way back I had to drive through a construction zone where most of the road was blocked off and only a narrow strip was left for the vehicles to pass by in either direction. While I was driving along the narrow strip next to the construction zone, I noticed a truck bearing down on me with no apparent intention of making way for my car to pass. I decided to swerve halfway out of the path of the truck, assuming that the truck driver, as was the unwritten rule of the road, would also give way to some extent. However, this driver refused to move even an inch out of the way. I found his arrogance irritating and pressed forward in the path I had chosen. I was sure that I could get him to move at least a little bit—in the West, I think this is called "chicken." Finally, as it became clear that he was definitely not going to swerve at all, I decided it was better to be chicken than dead, as I did not want to miss the opportunity to spend more time with Amma.

After the driver passed me, I spun my car around and gave chase. Enraged by his reckless and egoistic driving, I had decided to teach him a lesson. I overtook him and drove several kilometers ahead, increasing the distance between us. Then I turned the car around and got out, waiting for him to pass by. As I saw him approaching, I took a large stone from the side of the road and hurled it against his windshield, cracking it nicely. Then I got back in the car and sped away.

I returned to the ashram as fast as I could, eager to regale Amma with the tale of my heroic exploits. But when Amma heard the story, She was very upset and scolded me strongly. "Do you know how much it hurts me to hear what you have done? That poor driver will be forced to bear the expense of the new windshield." Then Amma posed a question for which I had no answer. "Would you have done the same thing if Amma had been sitting in the truck?"

When Amma said this, all the wind flew out of my sails. I hung my head in shame.

Amma is able to accept everyone as they are because She sees everyone as Her own Self. If we are not able to see our own Self everywhere, we can try to see our beloved Amma in everyone or see them as Amma's children. This will certainly bring about a shift in our perception that will reduce the number of conflicts and problems in our life and help us to be more patient and compassionate in all circumstances of life.

Chapter 4

The Supreme Dharma

Sometimes people ask Amma, "Isn't it enough to be a good person and lead a *dharmic* (righteous) life? If I am not harming anyone and I don't have any bad habits, why do I need to perform spiritual practices?"

To answer this question, first we have to understand more about dharma and what it really means to lead a dharmic life. According to the scriptures, there are actually a number of different types of dharma. In referring to a "dharmic life," the questioner is actually only referring to one type of dharma: to lead a morally upright, righteous life—not to cheat, not to steal, not to kill or harm others, to tell the truth, etc. Of course, everyone should observe these moral values, which are universally applicable to every society, culture and epoch. But simply observing moral values does not in itself constitute leading a wholly dharmic life. To do so, we have to have a deeper understanding of dharma and its various permutations.

The second type of dharma is specific to our faith or religious background. A Muslim has different observances and customs than a Jew, and a Christian has different obligations than a Hindu. For instance, Muslims are asked to pray five times a day, to fast during daylight hours for the entire month of Ramadan, and to make a pilgrimage to Mecca at least once in their life. Hindus might fast once or twice each week, take vows of silence, stay up all night during Shivaratri, wear a sacred thread, visit temples and chant their mantra. Christians and Jews have different observances particular to their faiths. To be a dharmic person in the second sense, we do not have to follow the observances of every faith; we only have to follow the observances of our particular faith. In some cases, though they have gone beyond the need for observing any customs and have transcended all differences—religion included—even the Self-realized Masters will follow the customs prescribed by their faith so as to set an example for others.

A third type of dharma relates to our position and role in society. For example, a soldier and a monk each have their own dharma. For a monk to take up arms in defense of his country would be totally inappropriate. But if a soldier refused to do the same, he or she would not be adhering to the relative dharma of his or her position. To adhere to our relative dharma is to perform sincerely and to the best of our ability the duties that have been entrusted to us. When everyone does this, society will function smoothly and everyone will prosper.

Finally there is the supreme dharma: the duty to realize our True Self, our oneness with God. Like the first type of dharma, this supreme dharma is common to everyone.

Amma says, "No matter who we are or what we are doing, the duties we perform in the world should help us reach the supreme dharma, which is oneness with the Universal Self. All living beings are one because life is one, and life has only one purpose. Owing to identification with the body and mind, one may think, 'To seek the Self and attain Self-realization is not my dharma; my dharma is to work as an actor or a musician or a businessman.' It is okay if one feels this way. However, we will never find fulfillment unless we direct our energy toward the supreme goal of life."

If we are sincerely following our dharma, we will begin to overcome our likes and dislikes, our selfishness, jealousy, pride and other negative qualities. For example, the dharma of a disciple is to follow the instructions of the Guru. Sometimes, the Guru will ask the disciple to do something he or she does not like to do.

Once a young man joined the ashram after having begun a career in filmmaking and photography. He told Amma that he would very much like to be Her personal videographer. Amma listened to his suggestion and then told him that She wanted him to work in the cowshed. This was the last thing this young man wanted to do, but since Amma asked him to do it, he obediently undertook the task of looking after the ashram's cows. However, his desire to make movies did not fall away easily. In addition to tending to their daily needs, he started making a documentary on the life of the cows; he would record their grazing, sleeping, milking and other activities. When Amma heard about this, She reminded him that the dharma of a seeker is to do whatever *seva* (selfless service) has been assigned to one, and to spend the rest of one's time in meditation, *mantra japa* (chanting the mantra), study and prayer—to do otherwise is like stepping out on the spiritual path and then sitting down in the middle of the road. Through following Amma's instructions, this young seeker was able to overcome his preferences and dedicate himself wholeheartedly to the work Amma had given him.

Like this, by pursuing our dharma sincerely, our mind will become more pure and more mature. When we have attained a greater degree of mental maturity, we will naturally take an interest in spirituality and the supreme dharma of Self-realization. At the same time, it is only spirituality that will give us the strength to adhere to dharma under all circumstances.

Take, for example, the case of Yudhishthira, who is said to have been the incarnation of the principle of dharma in a human form. Yudhishthira, the eldest of the five Pandava brothers and the rightful heir to the Kuru throne, was exiled to the forest for 12 years by his jealous cousin, Duryodhana, who had assumed the king's mantle in his stead. Though Duryodhana had won the Pandavas' exile through treachery, and all of his brothers urged Yudhishthira to return to the kingdom and wage war on Duryodhana and his brothers the Kauravas, Yudhishthira insisted on keeping his word and remaining in exile for the entire period of 12 years. Only when that period had expired did Yudhishthira agree to remove the unrighteous Kauravas from power and regain what was rightfully his.

It is only through understanding spiritual principles and performing spiritual practices that we will gain the right understanding and the right mental attitude in order to persevere in performing good actions no matter what kind of response we get in return.

Once Saint Eknath saw a scorpion floundering in a pool of water. He decided to save it by stretching out his finger, but the scorpion stung him. Eknath briefly withdrew his hand, wincing in pain. After a few moments Eknath again tried to rescue the scorpion from the water, but the scorpion stung him again. This went on for some time.

Finally an onlooker asked Eknath, "Why do you keep trying to rescue a scorpion knowing it will only sting you in return?"

Eknath explained, "It is the nature of the scorpion to sting; it is my nature to love. Why should I give up my nature to love just because it is the nature of the scorpion to sting?" Finally the scorpion, held in thrall by the power of Eknath's compassion, refrained from stinging him anymore, and Eknath happily retrieved the scorpion and placed it safely on the ground.

Only spirituality can give us the strength to go on loving and serving others, even when they only sting us in return. As the Buddha said, "Hatred does not cease by hatred at any time; hatred ceases by love—this is the eternal law."

When Amma was still a young woman, She was walking with another young lady from the village, collecting leftover scraps of food from the neighbors for Her family's cows. At that time many of the villagers used to harass Amma; they thought that rather than being a divine incarnation, She was just a lunatic. As they passed in front of one house, a man standing in the doorway called out loudly, "That Sudhamani is so strange, no wonder Her family can't find a husband for Her. Or is it that they can't afford a dowry? If they don't have the money, I'll pay for it. She just needs a husband to set Her straight..." The man went on talking like this as Amma and the other young woman passed by. Amma was totally unruffled by his comments, but the other woman, who knew Amma and had faith in Her as a divine being, was deeply pained by his words. As they walked on, Amma tried to console Her, saying that we must not be affected by the words of others, they are only displaying their own nature, etc. But the woman could not be comforted. She could not imagine how this man could be so needlessly cruel, and toward Amma most of all.

Shortly after that incident, as fate would have it, the man who had been heckling Amma was caught in a terrible storm on his fishing boat. Two of his family members drowned, and the boat sunk and was smashed against the beach. In the blink of an eye, his livelihood was destroyed. Unable to get help from any other source, this same man finally came to Amma begging for assistance. An ordinary person might have remembered this man's earlier cruelty and sent him away. Yet even though the ashram had very few resources at that time, Amma did everything She could to help him. Whatever money She had, She gave to him to help him get back on his feet.[3]

In the wake of the 2004 tsunami disaster, a similar story could be seen unfolding on a much grander scale. Many of the villagers in the district surrounding Amma's ashram lost everything that day. In the days after the disaster, Amma told Her senior disciple, Swami Amritaswarupananda, that She planned to dedicate $23 million for the relief and rehabilitation of the tsunami victims. Later, he said that when he first heard this, he couldn't believe his ears. "What!?" he asked Amma, flabbergasted. "23 million dollars! Where is the money going to come from?"

Amma was calm. She simply said, "It will come." There was so much certainty and firmness in Her voice. There was not even a hint of doubt. For a multi-national company to make a decision to invest 23 million dollars would take months. There would be rounds of board meetings, expert analysts would be called in to calculate the risks and potential gains. But for Amma, compassion is most important. Her decision just came forth, spontaneously. In a heartbeat, the decision was made. "It will come."

Though many of these same people had mercilessly teased Amma as a child, and even thrown stones at Her when She was a young woman, that did not give Amma pause even for an instant. From the moment the waters rushed in—and even though the ashram itself had suffered extensive material losses—Amma was wholeheartedly dedicated to helping the villagers regain

---

[3] It should not be misconstrued that Amma in some way caused this misfortune to befall him. Though Amma was totally unaffected, the other young woman's innocent heart was deeply wounded by the man's words. The man's hurtful words returned to him as a painful experience.

everything they had lost. It is only Amma's knowledge that She is one with Source of creation that allows Her to love and serve others no matter how She is treated in return.

As one of the first spiritual seekers to decide to live at Am-ma's feet, seeking refuge and guidance in Her alone, Swami Pranavam-ritananda Puri is one of Amma's senior disciples. As such, he has been in charge of various ashram branches at different times. The night before he was to leave Amritapuri for an extended period for the first time, Amma gave him a piece of advice he says he will never forget. "If you go with the conviction that no matter how much good you do to the world, no one will say anything good about you," Amma told him, "you will never be disappointed."

Here, Amma is pointing out that it is not only the action but the attitude with which we act that is important. When we perform good actions, we may expect to receive recognition or favors in return from those who are receiving our help. When we don't get the response we were expecting, we may lose our enthusiasm and even stop doing good actions. The following story illustrates this point.

Once a man from Mumbai came to see Amma in Amritapuri. Earlier, he had made a generous donation to the ashram. When he informed the line monitors that he was there to see Amma, they issued him a token and told him that he could go and have his lunch and relax, as he would have to wait a few hours before it was his turn to join the line and receive Amma's darshan. When the man heard this, he burst out angrily, "Don't you know who I am? I gave so much money to the ashram in Mumbai! How can you stop me like this?" The man was so offended that he left the ashram without even receiving Amma's darshan.

Even though this man had the good heart to donate gener-ously, he expected special treatment and recognition in return. The beauty of his good deed was spoiled by his incorrect attitude, and it even blinded him to the benefit of receiving Amma's darshan.

I remember another example of this type of giving from my very earliest days with Amma. At that time I was working in a bank and as there were no vegetarian restaurants nearby, I developed the habit of skipping lunch and dinner as well. After breakfast, I would only have some tea and snacks in the afternoon. At that time, during Her Krishna and Devi bhava darshan, Amma would give one or two spoonfuls of payasam (sweet rice pudding) to each person who came for darshan as *prasad*.[4] But whenever I went for Amma's Devi bhava darshan at night after returning from the bank, knowing how hungry I was, She would give me a lot of extra *payasam*. After that She would ask me to stay there and meditate for a while.

At that time there was another devotee who was very jealous of the attention Amma paid toward the first brahmacharis, especially me. One day he presented Amma with a real tiger-skin *asana* (meditation rug).[5] However, as Amma did not alter Her treatment of me and the other brahmacharis, one day he burst out in frustration, "There is only space for Brahmins here!" So saying, he retrieved the tiger-skin asana from the place where it

---

[4] Any item that the Guru has blessed is called prasad. Also, whatever is offered to the Guru or to God is sanctified and therefore becomes prasad.

[5] In ancient times, a tiger-skin asana was used by yogis for meditation. Tiger skin is said to retain the positive spiritual vibrations generated by the person using the asana; if one used an asana made of other materials, the vibrations might pass right through the asana and into the earth. Of course, now, as tigers have become an endangered species, no one is using them anymore. But in the early 1980s, while a rare and expensive item, they were still available. Of course, for a Self-realized Master like Amma, such material aids are totally irrelevant. Ignorant of this fact, this devotee felt he was doing a great favor for Amma.

had been stowed and left the ashram. After that he came to see Amma only rarely. Of course, the man's statement was absurd. Amma has never shown any preference toward anyone because of caste, religion or anything else. In fact Amma was not showing preference toward me, either. It was only that at that time there were very few of us around Amma who were interested in meditation and becoming brahmacharis; most of the people were householder devotees who wanted only to tell Amma their problems and go home. For those of us who liked to meditate, Amma would give special opportunities to sit by Her side.

Even though the man had presented Amma with a lavish gift in the form of this rare traditional asana, because he did not receive the reward he expected, not only was the beauty of his giving spoiled, he even revoked the gift itself.

Pride and egoism can spoil not only our good actions, but our good qualities as well. Once Amma commented that a particular brahmachari was very humble. The next day, Amma said that another brahmachari had a great deal of humility, when the first brahmachari was standing nearby. On hearing Amma's words he immediately protested, "Amma, how can you say that about him? I am so much more humble than he is!" In the heat of the moment, this brahmachari obviously didn't realize the irony of taking pride in his own humility.

Humility is a unique quality, in that the claim that one possesses it is certain evidence that one does not. Thus, it is probably the most elusive of all virtues. Amma says that a true seeker should not expect even one word of appreciation. Too often, humility is not renunciation of pride but the substitution of one pride for another—being proud that we are not proud. We should seek diligently to be humble but we should also realize that if we ever do achieve perfect humility we will be so unaware of ourselves by then that we will not even recognize ourselves as being humble.

Once the Buddha advised his disciples, "There are 80,000 different kinds of ignorance in the human mind. If you want to serve humanity, you must be prepared to accept 80,000 different kinds of abuse."

When Amma first launched the ashram's housing project, building and distributing free homes to the poor homeless, She sent many of the brahmacharis out to supervise and even carry out the construction work. When the brahmacharis returned to the ashram, some of them complained to Amma that one of the recipients of the new homes—who had been living in a ramshackle tin-and-cardboard hut—did not seem at all grateful for what was being given to him. Though he had no work of his own, he refused to help the brahmacharis in any way. He would just stand nearby smoking cigarettes and watching disinterestedly. One night, after the brahmacharis had poured concrete, they asked the future homeowner to water the concrete to help it cure overnight. His response was, "That's not my job and I don't want to do it."

The brahmacharis asked Amma, "Why should we bother to build homes for such people?"

Amma replied, "Children, it's your duty to build the homes. Furthermore, this person was just being himself. If he had acted any differently, he would be someone else." In other words, people just act according to their nature, and we should not expect them to act any differently.

If these brahmacharis did not have Amma to correct their attitude, they would certainly have lost their enthusiasm and motivation to serve the poor after being treated badly a few times. With Amma's guidance they were able to see the experience as an opportunity to practice action for action's sake and cultivate equanimity of mind—doing their duty without worrying about whether their efforts were met with appreciation or criticism.

If we perform charity or any kind of good deed while expecting to receive gratitude or recognition, we are creating more karma for ourselves, and—though it be good karma—we will have to experience the (positive) results of these actions. While the results of harmful or negative actions can be compared to being bound with an iron chain—as we are destined to experience the painful results of our negative actions—the results of good actions performed with a selfish attitude can be compared to being bound with a golden chain.

Whether we are bound with a golden chain or an iron chain, we are still in bondage. Though we will experience success, prosperity and pleasant experiences as a result of these actions, we will still be trapped in the cycle of birth and death.

There are those who dedicate their life to performing good actions and the appropriate *yagnas* (rituals) in order to gain entrance to heavenly realms upon their death. But even if they succeed, according to Sanatana Dharma, existence in heaven is not eternal. That is why in the *Katha Upanishad*, when Yama, the Lord of Death, offers the young boy Nachiketas entrance into the highest realm of heaven, promising him the greatest pleasures for a virtual eternity, Nachiketas refuses the offer and says he only wants Self-knowledge, which alone would grant freedom from the cycle of birth and death. Nachiketas knew that all pleasures—worldly or otherworldly—are temporary and ultimately flawed, and that when a soul's merit is exhausted, it will again have to descend to earth to take birth as a human being. Similarly, in the *Bhagavad Gita*, Lord Krishna declares,

te taṁ bhuktvā svargalokaṁ viśālaṁ
kṣīṇe puṇye martya-lokaṁ viśanti

Having enjoyed the vast world of heaven,
they returnto the world of mortals.

(IX.21)

Of course, this does not mean that we should give up performing selfless service because our attitude is not totally selfless; as long as we are performing actions with that goal in mind, our minds will become more and more expansive and in due course we will reach a state where our service is truly selfless.

Amma says, "Though we may not get the proper response from others for our good deeds, we should never give up doing good things. Even if no one else appreciates what we are doing, there will still be a positive effect."

Here, Amma is referring to the fact that any given action has at least two results: a visible result and an invisible result. A person may respond positively or negatively to our good deed; that is the visible result. But for every good deed we perform, irrespective of the visible result, we are accruing positive merit; that is the invisible result. So while the visible result can be positive or negative, the invisible result of a virtuous action is always positive. For example, when we feed a hungry person, the result we directly perceive is that the person's hunger is appeased. The invisible result is that we are gaining some positive merit for performing this good action.

Remembering that at least the invisible result of our positive actions will always be positive, and without placing too much importance on whether we receive external appreciation or recognition, we should always do our best to adhere to our dharma and perform dharmic actions.

There is a special kind of turtle that wipes its tail across the ground as it walks. The turtle does this in order to prevent potential predators from following its footprints. To an extent, this works. But certain predators have caught on to its technique and now, instead of looking for the turtle's footprints, they look for the pattern created on the ground by the swishing of its tail.

To progress spiritually and to ultimately break free of the bondage of birth and death, we perform good actions. But when we do the right thing with the wrong attitude, we are like this turtle. Our wrong attitude is like the tail that erases the impressions created by our good actions but leaves a mark of its own, creating more bondage for us. That is why Amma says that after doing something good, we should immediately forget about it.

If we turn the key in a lock to one side, it locks. When it is turned to the other side, it unlocks. Likewise, actions performed with the wrong attitude will lock us into *samsara* (the cycle of birth and death), while actions performed with the proper attitude will open the lock of samsara and set us free.

Part 2

The Makings of
a Blessed Life

"May the tree of our life be firmly rooted in the soil of love. Let good deeds be the leaves on that tree. May words of kindness form its flowers and may peace be its fruits."

– Amma

Chapter 5

Spiritual Living

In reading the scriptures without proper guidance or understanding, we may draw the mistaken conclusion that the five senses are somehow inherently evil. But by observing Amma, we can understand that it is not so. Amma shows us that we can use the same five senses in a positive way—in a way that facilitates, rather than hinders, our spiritual growth.

Amma uses Her ears to listen to the sorrows of the suffering people, Her speech to console and comfort them, and Her eyes to shed compassionate glances on all. No matter what our life's circumstances, we can all try to be committed to thinking good thoughts, hearing good things, speaking kind words and doing good actions.

One day in Amma's San Ramon Ashram during Her 2005 U.S. tour, a devotee's three-year-old boy, who was born by Amma's blessings, came to Her with a complaint. He stood in front of Amma and boldly declared, "I don't like anyone here in this ashram."

Instead of dismissing the comment as child's prattle, Amma took his complaint seriously. "Why, my son? Did someone here shout at you?"

"No," the boy replied.

Amma then asked, "Wouldn't you feel sad if the people here said they didn't like you?"

The boy agreed with that.

Then Amma imparted a lifelong teaching to the child—and to all the others who were observing the exchange, including the boy's father. Using Her hands for emphasis, Amma said, "In everything you hear, in everything you see, in everything you smell, in everything you eat…" Then, waving Her hand toward all the people in the hall, She continued, "In people everywhere…you should feel God in everything." With this, Amma managed to explain even to a three-year-old how the senses can be applied positively in our life.

Like this, Amma teaches us how to redirect our energy for a good purpose instead of suppressing it. This is a very important technique in spirituality. For example, if we try to dam a raging river, it is a very difficult process that may cause damage to the ecosystem and to ourselves, too. If we instead slightly redirect the river's flow at its source, the end result will be that the river reaches a totally different destination.

Amma never tells us to suppress our thoughts and desires. Instead, She very skillfully redirects the flow of our mind so that it flows toward God. When our mind flows toward God, naturally all our energy and actions will serve a higher purpose. Instead of leading a selfish life, we become more selfless and compassionate. Enjoyment is not wrong; it is just not good when it is only for ourselves. For example, it is fine for us to spend our time and money on some enjoyments. But, as Amma says, at least a portion of our time and resources should go for the sake of the poor and needy.

Actually, it is a very simple concept and process. But practically speaking, we need constant reminders and a perfect role model. This is where we can get the real benefit of being with a Master like Amma. You may be familiar with Amma's example of the Master being like a booster rocket that helps us to break free of the orbit of our negative tendencies and selfish desires. Recently, I read that a Russian solar sail crashed back to earth because of a failure in its booster rocket. If we depend on a physical booster rocket, we never know when it will fail us or run out of fuel. But the booster rocket of the Master will never fail us, because the Master has the inexhaustible fuel of unconditional love.

How can we use the example of Amma's life as a booster rocket? First, by spending time in Amma's presence we develop a love for Amma, or at least for the things She does. Seeing the life of self-sacrifice that She leads, we, too, start letting go of our infatuation with sense objects.

Amma tells the following story. Once, a rich man had a private interview with Amma. He used to sleep on a luxurious, king-size bed, so he thought that after giving darshan and straining Herself for so many hours, Amma would be using a nice, comfortable bed too. But when he found out that Amma always sleeps on the hard floor, he was shocked. He decided to sell his luxurious bed and donate the money to charity.

Once, a group of youngsters came to the ashram when Amma was giving darshan. Most of them were intoxicated, and one in particular vomited all over the floor right after having Amma's darshan. Devotees sitting near Amma all moved away in disgust; even his own friends couldn't stand to be near him. But Amma immediately got up from Her chair and cleaned the boy's face and chest with Her own sari. Then She started cleaning the mess on the floor with Her own hands. Soon the devotees came with a mop and a bucket of water. Seeing the depth of Amma's love and humility brought about a real change in the youngsters. They felt so remorseful that they gave up drinking altogether.

Amma shows us that our life is not meant simply for our own enjoyment. She shows us a higher purpose in life, and how to use our body, mind and senses to achieve it.

In the *Keno Upanishad*, there is a peace invocation that reads, "Let all my limbs be strong and healthy, Oh Lord. May my speech, breath, eyes, ears and all other organs be strong and healthy... May I never forget that Supreme *Brahman*, which pervades this whole Universe."

This means, "May my five senses not deceive me by giving me the shallow knowledge of forms and sound; may they be strong enough to penetrate the external names and forms and behold the Truth behind them."

Amma tells the following story. Once a businessman went to see a Guru. The businessman told the Guru that he had plenty of money, a loving wife, and obedient children, but still he was unable to experience any peace of mind. The Guru replied, "If you are interested, I will give you a mantra."

The businessman produced a huge bundle of keys and said, "Each of these is a key to a factory for which I am responsible. Where is the time for me to chant a mantra?"

The Guru patiently asked, "Do you take a shower every day?"

"Of course," the man replied.

"How far is the bathroom from your bed?" the Guru inquired.

"It's about 10 steps," he answered.

"On the way to the bathroom, what are you doing?"

"Nothing. I simply walk."

"So, on your way to the bathroom, why can't you just chant your mantra a few times?"

The businessman agreed that he could do that.

"And what about while you are taking your shower? Are you busy then?"

The businessman agreed that he could also chant his mantra in the shower.

Similarly the Guru advised the businessman that while brushing his teeth, eating his breakfast, and walking to his car he could mentally chant his mantra. The businessman sincerely followed the Guru's advice, and in due course he was able to chant his mantra during many of his daily activities.

The Roman philosopher Seneca said, "Everyone has time if he likes. Business runs after nobody; people cling to it of their own free will and think that to be busy is a proof of happiness." Especially in today's world, people often complain that they are too busy to do any spiritual practices or to lead a spiritual life. But just like the businessman in the story, if we look closely at our life, we will definitely find the time to remember God. No matter how busy we may be, we can find many short periods of time throughout the day when we have some free time, even if it is just a few minutes on a bus, waiting in line somewhere, or when we are engaged in some routine work, thus leaving the mind free to chant the mantra. Instead of trying to fill all our free time with some kind of entertainment or indulging in thoughts about the past and future, we should learn to convert at least some of our free time into quality time. While we are on hold on the phone, for example, we can try to be still within, remembering that our true nature is stillness and peace. If Amma is our Guru, we can remember a sweet experience we had with Her, or we can imagine that Amma is seated in our heart. If we are waiting in line at the post office, we can imagine that we are waiting in line for Amma's darshan. (But be careful not to hug the post-office clerk when he or she gives you your stamps!)

If we are not devotional in nature, we can simply observe our own breath, remaining conscious of every inhalation and exhalation. This in itself is a spiritual practice that will help to create more awareness within us.

While we are performing spiritual practices and deepening our understanding of spiritual principles, we should be especially careful how we make use of our free time. For instance, when we have a free evening or weekend, we can attend a satsang (meeting of spiritual aspirants) or do some volunteer work. If we do something spiritually useful with our free time, at least for that time our mind will be relatively pure, and we will be helping others as well. At the same time, we should be careful not to create new vasanas[1]. We can do this by reading spiritual books, visiting Amma's ashrams, and spending time with devotees or other spiritual aspirants. To a great extent, engaging in such activities will prevent the creation of more vasanas. The first step in eliminating or overcoming our vasanas is to remove ourselves from the places that bring out our vasanas. For instance, Amma says that if we are addicted to watching TV, we cannot keep a TV in our bedroom and then say we are not going to watch TV. The first step is to get the TV out of the room. It is much more difficult to avoid something when our senses come in contact with it. If we can avoid it completely, if we put ourselves in a place where there is less opportunity for the existing vasanas to manifest, we have a greater chance of success. Of course, if the vasana is strong we may not be able to remove it completely, but we can still try to regulate it; if we are unable to stop watching TV altogether, we can watch spiritual movies or something educational.

---

[1] Literally, vasana means "tendency". In this book, it is used to denote negative tendencies in particular. Ultimately, all tendencies must be transcended in order to attain Liberation, or Self-realization, but an important part of the process is to rid oneself of all negative tendencies and to actively cultivate positive tendencies.

We can also examine the routine activities we do every day and find ways to do them more consciously, to convert them into reminders of our true nature and the ultimate goal of our life.

How we wake up in the morning is very important. When we wake up in the morning, before putting our feet on the ground, let us give thanks to the earth for supporting and sustaining us. Before getting out of bed we should pray, "Oh Lord, let me not harm anyone today, be it in thought, word or deed. Let me do some good things for others today."

While taking our morning bath, we can remember to be grateful to Mother Nature for providing us water. We can take care not to use more water than we need, remembering that water is a precious resource. We can also remember that not everyone has access to water, and we can pray that everyone's needs are met.

Before eating, we can offer our gratitude to God for giving us food to eat. We can remember that there is so much sacrifice and effort involved on the part of other living beings in order to bring us this food. Also, we should be careful not to take more than we can eat. Wasting food is equal to disrespecting God and all the people who don't have anything to eat. Amma puts it bluntly: "Taking more food than we need is an act of violence." Recently I read a study on poverty worldwide that concluded that if you have food in the refrigerator, clothes on your back, a roof over your head and a place to lie down, you are wealthier than 60% of people in this world. Many of us take all of these things for granted; we consider them our birthright. But it is not so for the vast majority of human beings. In fact we are very fortunate to possess even these simple fundamental necessities. When we think about the plight of suffering people all over the world, how can we say our life is not blessed?

Amma says, "We usually do not count our blessings but are ever ready to complain. This attitude is wrong. God has given us so much in life—healthy bodies, sunshine, air and water. Yet, we do not express our gratitude toward God. We should try to cultivate a heart filled with gratitude and love for God."

One of the most important times of day is dusk. Amma says that worldly vibrations are very strong at that time because all living beings are thinking about their day-to-day lives and craving sleep. Amma says that if we do not do some kind of spiritual practice at this time, we will be adversely affected by all of these worldly vibrations. This is why Amma recommends that we chant or sing bhajans loudly at dusk rather than eating, sleeping or doing other extroverted activities. In this way, we can avoid negative thoughts, and the mind will become concentrated on God. Amma says it will even help to purify the atmosphere.

Traditionally, especially in Brahmin families, dusk is the time set aside for spiritual practice. The family goes to their puja room and prays and chants for at least half an hour. Nowadays, however, at 6:30 or 7:00 in the evening in India, all the box-office movies are shown on television. So what often happens is that the parents make sure the children are doing their prayers at that time so they can watch the evening movie in peace.

I have seen this when I visit houses of Amma's devotees in India. I remember visiting a house at precisely 6:30 p.m., and the parents had just sent the children to the puja room. But since I was there, they could not watch the movie. I could tell they were disappointed that I had come at that time, but they didn't want to tell me to go away. Later they themselves told me, "Swami, we tell our children to pray exactly from 6:30 p.m. to 7:00 p.m. The movie is shown only in half-hour episodes, so that is enough for us." Inwardly, I prayed to Amma and thanked Her that at least they didn't tell me to go away.

Amma has commented that even though people may have some interest in spirituality and some love for God, there are few indeed who would take Liberation even if it was offered to them. Amma jokes that even if God Himself were to come to our doorstep and offer us the Supreme Realization, we would say, "You know, Lord, this is a really fantastic movie I am watching. Can You come back when it's over?"

What we do before we go to sleep is also very important. Instead of watching a violent movie or reading a horror novel, we should try to read something with some moral or spiritual values. We can read a few pages of Amma's teachings or those of another Realized Master. We can also read from a scriptural text. There are many who insist that movies and media have no affect on a person's attitudes or behavior, but many psychologists will tell you that it is better to read something that will soothe and calm the mind, especially before going to bed.

Amma also advises that we should meditate for 10 minutes just before going to sleep and again for 10 minutes just after we wake up. It is for good reason that She says this; regular meditation has a subtle but very important effect. Amma says that different emotions produce different vibrations in and around us. Anger produces one type of vibration, lust produces another and motherly love produces yet another. *Mantrajapa* (chanting the mantra)and meditation produce a very beneficial vibration within us. Modern science has conducted many studies showing that meditation also has a very positive influence on our physical and mental health and even activates parts of the brain related to happiness and feelings of well-being. A study on the power of meditation at the University of Wisconsin measured the activity of these portions of the brain in ordinary people and contrasted it with the same part of the brain in Tibetan Buddhist monks. In the senior monks who had been meditating regularly for many years, their "happiness" indicator was actually off the top of the chart that had been generated by the University for the study. These monks were happier than the scientists had considered it was possible to be.

The ancient Sages placed a great deal of importance on performing spiritual practice before we start our day. In the *Srimad Bhagavatam*, as part of a description of the decay or spiritual and moral values in the Kali Yuga, or the Age of Materialism (of which we are now in the midst), Sage Shuka says that merely to "take a bath without any other morning routine will be enough to appear for the day." Don't most of us think in exactly this way? Especially if we are in a hurry, we will simply have a quick shower and dash out the door with a piece of toast in our hand. But what the Sages are reminding us is that our mind needs a morning bath as well. This internal cleanliness can only be attained through meditation and other spiritual practices.

Some people ask why there are so many external rituals and ceremonies in Sanatana Dharma if God is within. Such people wonder, "How do we find the God inside if we are always looking outside?"

If such people would close their eyes for two minutes and try to find God within, I think they would have the answer to their question. Looking within is not as simple as it sounds. Our minds are extremely extroverted in their tendencies; if we launch a direct attack on the mind, immediately trying to withdraw our senses and focus inward, the mind will revolt; our mental restlessness will increase tenfold.

There is a verse in the *Katha Upanishad*:

parāñci khāni vyatrṇat svayambhū
stasmāt parāṅpaśyati nāntarātman

*The self-existent Supreme Lord inflicted an injury
upon the sense organs in creating them with outgoing
tendencies; therefore a man perceives only outer objects
with them and not the inner Self.*

(II.i.1)

Amma says that even though God is within, our mind is not looking within. The purpose of the external forms of worship is, in essence, to trick the mind into focusing on God. We let the mind flow outward, as it likes to do, but we control the object of our attention. Slowly, with practice, we can shift our attention inward.

In India, mothers of young children have an interesting way of coaxing a young child to eat. We all know that it is difficult to convince toddlers to eat when we want them to. So what these mothers do is, rather than calling their children to come and eat, they offer them something else to do. The mother will tell the child, "Come, darling, let us go and look at the moon." And while pointing out the moon and commenting on its features, as the child's attention is totally absorbed in the moon, the mother will pop a morsel of food into the child's mouth. Or the mother will take the child to a park and push him in a swing. And each time the child swings back toward the mother, she will feed the child a bite of food. But the child does not feel he is eating; he feels that he is swinging or looking at the moon.

External forms of worship are like this. Even hatha yoga is an external form of worship. In hatha yoga we concentrate on the position of the body, but the real purpose is to calm and concentrate our mind. Similarly, some people like to meditate by focusing on their breath. But again, the desired result is to quiet the mind. And since the mind is so intimately connected with the body and the breath, either of these techniques can work very well—without the mind feeling that it has come under attack.

When we are doing *archana* (worship)[2], a *puja* (sacred ritual) or a *homa* (fire ceremony), or meditating on a picture of our Guru or beloved deity, we are focusing our attention on what is in front of us. In that way we are able to withdraw the eyes, the ears and the other sense organs from all other things. Slowly, this will help us to develop more concentration. Rather than the senses reaching out toward many different objects, we are trying to focus them on one object—not just any object but an object with divine qualities, so we are simultaneously cultivating a pure heart. As the mind gets more concentrated, it becomes easy to focus within. That is the purpose of all these external rituals. Even though it is external, it is a process of slowly turning within.

Even if we only sit for spiritual practices for 20 minutes a day, we should not feel that we have no chance to lead a spiritual life. In Her 2005 Guru Purnima address, Amma offered the following simple practices that each of us can incorporate into our life, in order to lead a life in keeping with Her teachings:

1) A day of silence once per week. This can be observed together with meditation, mantra japa or fasting.

2) If you are angry with someone, make a phone call or write a kind and loving letter to him or her.

3) Once a week, make a vow: "I won't get angry with anyone today." We may fail and get angry with others, but we should continue our efforts without getting discouraged.

---

[2] In this book and at Amma's ashram, "archana" typically refers to the chanting of the Sri Lalita Sahasranama, the 1000 Names of the Divine Mother.

4) Create a spiritual timetable, listing things to practice and qualities to develop. Look at it every morning and follow the schedule. Amma points out that this timetable functions like a security alarm, which will warn us when troublemakers enter our premises.

Amma says that leading a spiritual life means leading our normal life with a spiritual attitude. In fact, most of our actions can become a spiritual practice. One of the most important spiritual practices is to cultivate positive qualities such as kindness, patience, compassion and love. If we look closely at our life, we will find that we have many opportunities to cultivate and express these qualities throughout our day.

In the Bhagavad Gita, Lord Krishna says,

ne 'hā bhikramanāśo 'sti pratyavāyo na vidyate
svalpam apy asya dharmasya trāyate mahato bhayāt

In this (spiritual path) there is no loss of attempt;
nor is there any adverse effect. The practice of even a
little of this dharma protects one from great fear.

(II.40)

Generally, the efforts we put forth in the world have two fundamental flaws. One such flaw is that if we do not achieve our goal for one reason or another, all the effort we put forth toward that end will have been wasted. For instance, we labor for months in the fields to produce a harvest. But if a cyclone strikes before harvesting time, we will have to start all over from scratch.

The second fundamental flaw is that our efforts may produce other than the intended result. If we take medicine for an illness, it may or may not be effective. At the same time, we might be allergic to the medicine. Thus, our effort failed to produce the desired result, and, in fact, produced a different result, which is contrary to what we hoped for.

In this verse, Krishna is telling us that efforts put forth on the spiritual path are not subject to the same fundamental flaws inherent in all other efforts. Just as we will always gain nourishment from eating a healthy meal, even the smallest effort put forth in spiritual practice or applying the spiritual principles in our life will certainly benefit us. This is another law of the universe, as unwavering as the law of karma. Understanding this truth, we should never hesitate to turn to spirituality, no matter how advanced in years we may be, and we should never think of giving up our efforts, or despairing that it has all been for naught. When we perform spiritual practice, we will benefit; we must benefit. This is a universal law.

Chapter 6

Reverse Engineering – Expanding the Mind with Selfless Service

In his famous poem "The Waste Land" poet T.S. Eliot describes modern life as morally and spiritually vacant. At one point in the poem, the narrator observes a seemingly unending line of people crossing over London Bridge on their way to work. Their motions are so mechanical and their lives appear so devoid of meaning that Eliot refers to them as the Living Dead, saying, "I had not thought death had undone so many."

The scriptures of Sanatana Dharma say that whoever lives just for one's own sake without helping others is not really living; such a person is merely alive, like an animal. A person in a coma may be alive, but is he or she really living? Similarly, a person who leads a purely selfish existence is simply alive. In the *Bhagavad Gita*, Lord Krishna refers to such people as thieves because they always take from the world and never give anything in return. Amma says that as long we go on taking from others, we remain a beggar. But when we begin to give to others, we become a king. Real living begins when we start to help and serve others, when we show compassion.

There was a very successful businessman who ran a tight ship at his company. For 10 years, one of his employees had arrived to work each day at 9:00 a.m. on the dot. He had never missed a day of work or even been late. Consequently, on one particular day when 9:00 a.m. rolled by without this employee's arrival, it caused a sensation in the office. All work ceased, and the boss himself, looking at his watch and muttering, came out into the corridor.

Finally, precisely at 10:00 a.m., the employee showed up, clothes dusty and torn, his face scratched and bruised, his glasses bent. He limped painfully to the time clock, punched in, and croaked, "Sorry I'm late, but I tripped and rolled down two flights of steps in the subway. Nearly killed myself."

All the boss could say was, "It took you a whole hour to roll down two flights of stairs?"

Though the boss was a brilliant businessman, he lacked the fundamental human quality of compassion. Even though he appeared to have accomplished so much, he could not even respond humanely to one who had served him so sincerely for so long.

Selfishness has become so prevalent that we need a truly striking example of selflessness like Amma in order to inspire us. Actually, we have one quality in common with Amma. We are both incorrigible but in different ways. We are incorrigibly selfish, and She is incorrigibly selfless. If Amma doesn't give darshan on any particular day, She doesn't feel worthy of eating. Whereas if we don't have any work, we feel that it is a good opportunity to eat an extra meal and have a nice nap. While we are only interested in finding ways to reduce our suffering, Amma voluntarily suffers for the sake of Her children.

I recall an incident that took place at Amma's ashram in India many years ago. It was Vijaya Dashami, a festival day for the Goddess of Knowledge, Saraswati. On this day, many devotees bring their children to the ashram for the writing ceremony wherein Amma initiates children into their formal studies. From 9:00 in the morning until noon, there were special prayers, bhajans, and Amma performed the writing ceremony for hundreds of children. When one particular child came for Amma's darshan, the child's mother told Amma that her daughter was always feverish and vomiting; and she prayed for Amma's help in curing her.

After all the writing ceremonies were over, Amma went to Her room, which was just a small hut at that time, and immediately fell ill. She started vomiting repeatedly and was running a very high fever. Amma commented that it was due to the illness that She had taken from the child. She said that this child had been suffering from this illness for many lifetimes, but Amma could exhaust the karma for her in just a short amount of time.

All of Amma's close disciples came to Her room and were very worried about Her condition. In a short while, Amma was scheduled to go back to the darshan hall and give darshan to all the devotees awaiting Her blessing on that auspicious day. Amma said that She was doubtful that She could make it. One of the brahmacharis went to the temple and announced to all the devotees that Amma was sick and that the afternoon darshan would unfortunately have to be cancelled. Hearing this news, the devotees were crushed and shocked, as Amma had never cancelled a darshan due to illness. For one of the women devotees, the pain of not being able to have Amma's darshan was so unbearable that she started sobbing loudly. Her crying became an intense wail of sorrow and anguish.

The hall was quite a distance from Amma's hut, so it is unlikely that She could have physically heard this woman's cry, but Amma definitely heard it in Her heart. In that instant, forgetting all the nausea, feverishness, headache and exhaustion She had been feeling just a moment before, Amma suddenly shot up out of Her bed and raced to the hall to console Her child. She then proceeded to sit and give darshan well into the evening.[3]

While most of us suffer due to our own past actions, True Masters like Amma suffer voluntarily so that others do not have to suffer—they take the results of our past actions on themselves. In fact, one of the 108 Names of Amma, chanted daily at Amma's ashrams and by Her devotees around the world, can be translated as, "She who is happy in exchanging heaven for hell for the relief of others."

As selflessness increases, the ego within us naturally decreases, and our inherent innocence shines forth. But we have to work to maintain that innocence—if we do not perform regular spiritual practices and take care to cultivate good thoughts, our dormant negative tendencies may rise up at any time and pull us down into unhealthy habits and thought patterns.

Readers of *Ultimate Success* may remember the story of the devotee whose son Amma permitted to establish a teashop on the ashram grounds many years ago. There is now another chapter, or you could say a new ending, to his story.

Even though the devotee was already advanced in years, he was so innocent that Amma used to call him Baby Krishna. But when Amma asked this devotee's son to relocate his teashop due to space constraints, this devotee lost all his innocence. When he argued with Amma that his son should be allowed to keep his teashop on the ashram grounds, Amma very compassionately said he could have some more time to find a new location. In

---

[3] In fact, to this day Amma has never cancelled a darshan program due to illness since She began giving darshan over 30 years ago. With that in mind, it appears that on this occasion Amma commented that the darshan would be cancelled only to increase the longing in the hearts of the devotees.

the meantime, however, a peepal tree, which is considered to be sacred, sprouted up in a crack in the wall of the shop. It is a commonly held belief in India that wherever a peepal tree sprouts, worldly and moneymaking activities will not flourish.

Knowing this, one day this devotee poured boiling water on the little peepal sapling, hoping it would die and therefore his son might not have to move the shop. The next day when he went for Amma's darshan, She asked him out of the blue, "My son, what did you do to that poor tree? You cannot destroy it because I have already made a *sankalpa* (divine resolve) that it will live for many years."

After this, the devotee became even angrier with Amma and stopped coming to see Her. He even began to spread false rumors about Amma, and for a long gap of 15 years, this devotee never came to see Amma. It took a natural disaster to bring him back to Her.

In December 2004, when the tsunami struck, many whole villages took shelter in the refugee camps Amma had established at Her university campus across the backwaters from the ashram. Amma visited the refugee camps many times, and on one occasion She met the devotee She used to call Baby Krishna, who had by then become old and frail. Amma went to his bed, stroked his head compassionately, inquired about his health, and assured him that the ashram would extend all the help required to his family.

As fate would have it, this elderly devotee passed away just two months later. At that time, Amma remarked that his earlier innocence and devotion made Her think about him and want to see him one more time before he left his body.

Here it is worth remembering Amma's words: "Even if we do 100 bad things and just one small good thing, Amma will always remember that one good thing and not the bad ones, whereas the world will remember only our mistakes, even if we do 100 good things and only one small bad thing."

I once read a story about three skydivers whose parachutes got tangled in mid-air. For a moment, it seemed as though all three of them were doomed, but then one of the skydivers realized that his parachute and body weight seemed to be causing the biggest problem, so he removed his parachute and plummeted to his death. As a result, the other two people could cut free his parachute from theirs, and they were saved.

Just think of the courage and selflessness it took to do such a thing. We are all living like people whose parachutes are entangled. Nobody is willing to sacrifice his or her own interest, so everyone suffers.

In so many circumstances of life we are unconsciously making a choice to help ourselves rather than others. This is, in a way, understandable. In the modern world, instant personal gratification is considered by many to be the very goal and purpose of life. But imagine the state of the world if Nature functioned by this principle. Amma says that human beings can learn a lot by observing Mother Nature: "For example, take an apple tree. It gives all its fruits to others, taking nothing for itself. Its very existence is for other living beings. Likewise a river; it washes away everyone's dirt, expecting nothing. It willingly accepts all impurities and returns purity sacrificing everything for others.

"Children, each and every object in this world teaches us sacrifice. If you observe closely, you find that all of life is a sacrifice. Each one's life is a story of sacrifice. The husband sacrifices his life for the wife, and the wife sacrifices hers for the husband; a mother for her children and the children for their family. Each one of us is sacrificing our life in one way or another. Without sacrifice there is no world."

In addition to spiritual practices like meditation, archana and bhajans, Amma encourages all of Her children to engage in selfless service: "When we do something selflessly for others without expectation, we become more expansive. Expansiveness is to experience the feeling that the Self in us is the Self in all. This is the goal of all spiritual practices. Expansiveness is God."

Here, Amma is saying that if we want our minds to be expansive, first our actions must become expansive. In a way, it is a sort of reverse engineering. Mahatmas like Amma are established in their oneness with all of creation—thus, they feel inspired to try to uplift suffering humanity. For us, it can be the other way—if we try to uplift suffering humanity, eventually we can come to experience our unity with all of creation.

One of the first major projects in the ashram's tsunami relief work was the construction of temporary shelters about a mile down the beach from the ashram. After the tsunami, so many people simply had nowhere to go, nowhere to sleep. The ashram housed many in its nearby university, and many others were put up in the local government schools. But as the winter holidays were coming to an end, the government indicated the people must leave so the schools could resume their classes. Thus, it became imperative that the temporary shelters be finished immediately.

The brahmachari in charge of the construction worked day and night. Each time Amma would call to check on the shelters' progress, he would be there working—midnight, 2:00 a.m., 4:00 a.m. At one point, Amma told him to get some sleep, but he said he could not, as he knew that every hour the shelters remained incomplete would be another hour that the tsunami victims would have no place to rest their heads.

About this brahmachari, Amma later commented, "Because he was so identified with the suffering of others, he was able to transcend his physical needs." She then added, "A mother never tires of taking care of her children because she considers them her own."

A few years back a Western tourist, who didn't know anything about Amma, passed through the ashram. He had heard that She hugs people while dressed up as the Divine Mother, and he wanted to see for himself. After checking in, the people in the foreign office told him to go to the seva desk where everyone gets assigned a job to help maintain the ashram. A brahmachari standing nearby overheard the conversation that took place there. The seva coordinator asked him, "Well, we have sweeping and pot-washing. Which one would you like to do?"

The man replied, "Umm, no thanks."

"What do you mean 'No thanks'?" the seva coordinator asked.

The visitor replied, "Sorry, but I'm not interested in doing any work."

"Well, Amma suggests that everyone here contribute a little bit of their time towards the upkeep of the ashram."

"Well, then maybe I came to the wrong place!" The man started getting angry, so the seva coordinator didn't push him any more. The man then went over to see Amma giving darshan, and the brahmachari who had been standing nearby followed him and started talking to him. "Aren't you going for darshan?" the brahmachari asked.

"No," the visitor said stoically, "I'm just going to watch." He watched with increasing curiosity until the end of the afternoon darshan, and as Amma climbed the stairs to Her room, he said, "Pretty impressive sitting all this time. But what is this Devi Bhava thing?"

"Oh, that's tonight," the brahmachari replied.

The visitor was surprised to hear this. "You mean to say that She's coming out again today?"

"Of course," the brahmachari said. "In just a couple of hours. Then She sits all night long until the last person comes."

The visitor couldn't believe this, but then he saw it with his own eyes that night. And when Devi Bhava was over at 7:00 the next morning, he ran into the same brahmachari once more. "That was amazing," the visitor told him. "So, She does this every single month?"

The brahmachari replied, "Hey, not every month—every day! Darshan every day and Devi Bhava twice a week!" Hearing this, the visitor was in a daze. He didn't quite know how to process that.

Shortly after that, Amma came back out of Her room and started doing "brick seva." At that time the main prayer hall was being built by hand by Amma and the ashram residents. Amma had taught all of the ashram residents how to make bricks by mixing sand and cement in the right proportion, and everyone was asked to make 10 bricks each day. As always, Amma worked right alongside the ashram residents in making the bricks and then laying them in place. Often, She would start this work almost immediately after giving darshan for hours on end. [4]

---

[4] Today, as part of the tsunami relief work, almost all of the ashram residents and many visitors from across India and abroad spend six or more hours each morning doing modern-day "brick seva." Most of the houses being reconstructed by the ashram in the wake of the disaster are not reachable by road. Thus it takes long hours and lots of help to move the bricks from the nearest road to the site of the new home. Each new house requires 13,000 bricks. In the ashram's immediate vicinity alone, more than 1,400 (of a total of 6,200) new houses are being built for tsunami victims. That's more than 18 million bricks that must be passed by hand by the ashram residents and visitors. However, inspired by Amma's example, the ashramites are undaunted as they work tirelessly under the hot sun and

On this occasion, after having just given darshan for 14 hours, Amma led the ashram residents in manual labor for a few more hours. By now, the man was completely confused. The next day he seemed to be in a stupor as he watched Amma give darshan again.

Later that week the seva coordinator approached the brahmachari who had spoken with this visitor. "Know what happened to that guy who didn't want to do any seva? This morning he came in like a little mouse and said, 'Excuse me, sir, but can I please have a seva assignment?'" This visitor later became one of the most dependable pot-washers in the ashram.

Amma says, "The beauty and charm of selfless love and service should not die away from the face of this earth. The world should know that a life of dedication is possible, that a life inspired by love and service to humanity is possible."

Let each of us in our own small way do whatever we can to ensure that Amma's wish is fulfilled. It need not be anything dramatic. When enough people do small things, it makes a big difference.

Shortly after the tsunami, Amma's devotees in Houston, Texas organized a tsunami-relief fundraiser. The event consisted of an Indian dinner and an evening of classical Indian music. Through hosting this one event, these devotees were able to meet their goal of raising $25,000 for Amma's tsunami-relief fund. Later, one of the organizers told me, "When I heard that Amma had pledged $23 million worth of relief work, I had the idea to raise $25,000 toward this goal, or 1/1000th of the total amount. If Amma's devotees around the world can organize 1,000 simple fundraisers like this, we can raise the entire amount." $23 million may seem like an impossible amount of funds to raise, but when we

pouring rain. By September 27th, 2005, Amma's 52nd birthday, 1,200 new homes had already been completed and distributed.

hear this man's innocent, optimistic perspective, it doesn't seem so hard to believe after all.

When a group of journalists asked Amma how She could possibly pledge such a large sum for tsunami relief, Amma replied, "My children are my strength." She was not speaking only about the brahmacharis, brahmacharinis and other ashramites who work up to 15 hours a day without receiving any pay, dedicated to helping as many people as possible as quickly as possible. Referring to Her millions of devotees around the world, Amma said, "I have many good children.

They all do what they can." She went on to describe how even small children make dolls or statues and sell them so that they can give the earnings to their beloved Amma. "Some children," Amma said, "when presented with money on their birthday or when their parents tell them that they can have an ice cream, say that they would like to give that money to Amma instead, telling their parents how Amma can use it for supporting poor children. Other children come up to Amma and offer their savings, saying that it can be used to buy pens for poor students. Amma doesn't want to accept this—as other children who have nothing to offer may then feel sad—but when Amma sees the goodness of their hearts, She has no choice. The government alone cannot do everything. Would these children give this money to the government with the same love as they would give it to Amma?"

Once a man with basically no spiritual background at all came to see Amma during one of Her foreign tours. The man was a professional motorcycle racer, a chain smoker and a heavy drinker. But when Amma arrived, he came to see Her out of curiosity, simply drawn to Her picture on the tour brochure. He said that merely upon entering the hall, he felt such an overwhelming wave of spiritual energy that he couldn't remain inside. Instead, he decided to do some seva outside as he saw the example of selfless service that Amma was setting. He said that the only useful thing that he could do was driving. So he shuttled people to and from the train station near the hall. Each time he picked up somebody and took them back, he could see the vast difference in their facial expression after having Amma's darshan, and a sense of satisfaction welled up in his heart.

Toward the end of his seva, the man went to the train station and picked up a boy with cerebral palsy in a wheelchair. There was such a look of sorrow and despair on the boy's face that the man felt a great deal of compassion for him. Later, the man took the boy back to the station after his darshan and helped him out of the van into his wheelchair. Their eyes met. Though the boy could not speak, the man could see the difference in the boy's face. It was aglow with so much vitality and joy, as though his life had started afresh. Tears of gratitude rolled down the speechless boy's cheeks, and he tried to extend his crooked arms toward the driver in appreciation of the one who had enabled him to receive this touching experience. Suddenly, the man felt an overwhelming flood of tearful joy welling up from deep within, and he burst out crying like a small child. Embracing the handicapped boy in his wheelchair, the two of them cried in each others' arms for a long time. After this experience, the man said he felt a deep abiding peace for days.

All this man did was to serve selflessly in a capacity that he already knew how to do, but by Amma's grace he was able to experience profound bliss—something that would normally take lifetimes of spiritual practice. Today he is a totally changed man, having given up all his bad habits in exchange for the sweet bliss of Amma's love.

Being one with the Supreme Being, Amma doesn't need us to wash pots or chop vegetables at Her programs. She doesn't need us to help with the ashram's selfless-service projects. She, in fact, doesn't need us to serve others at all. She offers us the opportunities to do such things because of the infinite good She knows such actions, if done with love, care and sincerity will provide us—the expansion they will bring to our minds. Many years ago, when the ashram first began undertaking large-scale social service projects, Amma commented, "Actually, I am not interested in building up a big ashram or in having an orphanage or an engineering institute or a hospital. I am doing all these things only for the devotees who are going to be here." Now, Amma's institutions are giving thousands upon thousands a chance to grow spiritually through selfless service.

Amma says, "Selfless service has great importance in one's spiritual development. Through selfless service, one can become purified and fully prepared or fit for Realization."

Let us pray to Amma that even though we may be totally ignorant of spirituality, that She at least give us the strength to perform selfless actions with a pure heart, slowly expanding our minds. If we at least make sincere efforts according to our own capacity, She will certainly reward us with the experience of inner bliss and guide us to the final goal of realizing the source of that bliss, or God, within our hearts.

Chapter 7

Leaving the Buffaloes Behind – Letting Go of Likes and Dislikes

The scriptures say that there is a pre-established harmony in creation. Even though animals kill other animals for food, they are only following the natural food chain designed by God, or Mother Nature. For us, to hunt and kill an animal is a sport. But if an animal kills a human being, the animal is not considered a terrific athlete. Instead, we say the animal is a vicious man-eater, and we kill it. Yet only human beings create disharmony in creation. We plunder and destroy Mother Nature, pollute the atmosphere and commit all sorts of crimes, thus creating chaos in the world.

The primary reason human beings act in this way is what the scriptures call *raga-dvesha* (likes and dislikes). Our whole life—almost everything we do—is propelled by our likes and dislikes. We want to get or possess what we like, and we want to avoid or get rid of what we don't like. It can be an object, a person or a situation. In order to accomplish these ends, people are willing to go to any extent, caring very little for moral and spiritual values. The phrase, "It's a dog-eat-dog world," is commonly accepted not as a description of the animal kingdom but of the nature of human society.

When a physician prescribes a medicine, it is not enough if he or she just knows that a particular medicine has the capacity to treat a disease. He or she should also know what side-effects the drug may cause to the patient. Similarly, when we want to fulfill a desire, we probably have a good idea about which action we could perform to fulfill that desire, but we don't stop to think about how the action will affect the other aspects of our life. This is why our experience is both pleasurable and miserable; it is the result of our efforts to fulfill our desires as well as the unforeseen consequences of those efforts.

Most people never even step back and question their incessant attempts to acquire what they like and avoid what they dislike. But if we analyze our own likes and dislikes, we can see that there is, in fact, no logic in them. For example, one person likes to smoke, whereas another person cannot even stand the smell of cigarettes. Some people love to drink whiskey, but others become nauseous if they take even a single sip. Escargot is a delicacy to half the world and a revolting prospect to the other half. One person likes something very much, and another person dislikes the very same thing. Moreover, the same person may dislike a certain thing at one point in his or her life and then later on like it very much. If happiness was the intrinsic nature of these objects, wouldn't they give happiness to everyone all the time?

Recently, I read a study conducted in the United States that showed that to some extent, money can buy happiness. However, the amount of money one has is not the determining factor. Rather, the study showed that the more money one has in relation to one's peers, the happier one tends to feel. That is to say, a person who earns $30,000 a year can be happier than a person who earns $100,000 a year, if the poorer person's peers make only $20,000 a year, while the wealthier person's peers earn about the same amount that he or she does. This means that the happiness these people feel is not derived from the amount of money they make but from a feeling of being more successful than those around them. How deep—and how permanent—can such happiness be?

If there is no logic behind our likes and dislikes, it means that we, the most intelligent beings on earth, are leading an illogical or irrational life. That is why the scriptures refer to worldly knowledge as inferior and spiritual knowledge as superior. The only thing in the world that can only and always benefit us is the knowledge of our True Self. Amma is here to help us gain this supreme knowledge, which is the only way to escape from the cycle of birth and death. What is this knowledge? It is the knowledge that we are one with God, who is all-knowing, all-powerful and all-pervasive.

Adi Shankaracharya points out in *Viveka Chudamani,* or *The Crest Jewel of Discrimination,* that animals routinely lose their lives due to being enslaved by any one of the five senses. A deer meets with its death due to its attraction to a particular sound that hunters make—moving closer to the sound brings the deer within range of the hunters' weapons. The moth is drawn to the light of the flame and is burnt by its heat. The honeybee diligently labors to collect pollen and produce honey, only to be killed by human beings who want the fruit of its labor. The elephant is mesmerized by the touch of another elephant, and together they fall into a deep ditch from which there is no escape. If animals can lose their life pursuing just one sense, Shankaracharya asks, what can be the fate of human beings who are enslaved by all five senses? Amma tells the following story.

A man wandering through a foreign city looking for entertainment enters an illicit guesthouse. Standing in the lobby, he sees three doors before him. Behind the door on the left is a club serving alcohol and other drugs. Behind the door in the center is a prostitute's chambers. Behind the door on the right is the office where the guesthouse profits are kept. Remembering his wife at home, the man says to himself, "I better not go to a prostitute. And I should not take illegal drugs, either. But what's the harm in having a few drinks?" Thinking thus, the man enters the club and has several drinks. Later, in an intoxicated state, he is less hesitant to take drugs. After taking the drugs, he leaves the club in a totally wild state. Seeing the prostitute's chambers, he no longer thinks it is such a bad idea to go inside. On his way out of the guesthouse, he robs the office. Finally, the man is caught by the police and sent to prison.

In the *Bhagavad Gita*, Lord Krishna declares,

dhyāyato viṣayān puṁsaḥ saṅgas teṣū 'pajāyate
saṅgāt saṁjāyate kāmaḥ kāmāt krodho 'bhijāyate
krodhād bhavati saṁmohaḥ saṁmohāt smṛtivibramaḥ
smṛti bhraṁśad buddhināśo buddhināśāt praṇaśyati

In the person who dwells upon objects, an attachment is born toward those objects. From attachment is born desire and from desire, anger is born. From anger comes delusion, and from delusion comes the loss of memory. Because of the loss of memory, the mind becomes incapacitated, and when the mind is incapacitated, the person is destroyed.

(II.62-63)

Here Krishna is explaining how our deep attachments to the objects of the world lead to our destruction. As a practical example, suppose a man walks to work each day. On the way, he passes many strangers; some he sees each day, while others he sees only once and never again. One day, he happens to notice an attractive woman who is also on her way to work. The next day, he sees the same woman again, and before long he finds himself looking forward to seeing her during his commute. One day he works up the courage to talk to her and ask her out on a date. In a very short time he falls in love with her and feels that he cannot live without her. Before meeting him, the woman was already being courted by another man. This creates an intense rivalry between the two men. One day a fight breaks out between them, and in the end they are each charged with attempted murder of the other. Needless to say, neither one of them wins the loyalty of the woman of their dreams.

We use our power of discrimination in some situations in life, but we don't apply it enough with respect to the sense organs. We spend most of our lives simply fulfilling the desires of our sense organs, often even becoming a slave to them. But if we observe Amma, we can see that it is possible for humans to lead a much more sublime life. Even from Her childhood, Amma never allowed Herself to become enslaved by the objects of the world; all Her energy was directed toward the service of suffering humanity. An ordinary person is controlled by his or her sense organs, whereas a Realized Master like Amma controls them.

To put it another way, both an arrested person and the president of the country will be surrounded by many police officers. While the arrested person is under the control of the police officers, the president has them at his or her command. Our goal should be to gradually approach this state of total control over our mind and our senses.

Let us take the simple example of food. There are cases where people will even go to the extent of getting a divorce, simply because their spouse doesn't cook tasty food. Does it sound unbelievable? I know of a man who could not stand his wife's cooking, and he used to go out for dinner every night at a nearby restaurant. He was served by the same waitress every night, and finally they fell in love and the man left his wife for the waitress. They lived happily ever after until the waitress left the man for another customer. Ultimately, the man found himself a twice-divorced bachelor who no longer felt comfortable in his favorite restaurant. All his troubles started from the desire for tasty food!

At Amma's ashram in San Ramon, California, every Saturday evening there is a satsang meeting followed by a potluck dinner. The dinner is renowned for being delicious, and being available for a small donation, it is also the best deal in town. It is so good that there was a man who used to come to the ashram only for the dinner. He would not attend the spiritual talk, meditation or bhajans but would show up only at 8:00 p.m. sharp for the dinner. He considered his wife a very bad cook, and the dinner at San Ramon Ashram was the highlight of his week. The man continued like this for months, and finally the time came for Amma to spend two weeks at the ashram, as She has done every June for the past 18 years. The man was not interested in meeting Amma, but he did not want to miss his favorite dinner of the week. One of Her programs happened to be on a Saturday, so he found himself at the ashram while Amma was giving darshan. Just as he was finishing his dinner, someone happened to offer this man a darshan token that would allow him to join the line immediately. As this man had an appreciation for things that were free and convenient, he decided to go for darshan. He thought of asking Amma to bless his wife so that She would become a better cook or at least to instruct the residents of San Ramon Ashram to offer their community dinner more than once a week.

Much to his surprise, the man was very touched by Amma's darshan, and he did not ask Her for anything at all. From the following week, he began attending the entire Saturday evening program, and he even helps to serve the evening meal. Now, only after everyone else has eaten their fill does this man agree to take a plate for himself.

So while overindulgence in the senses most often leads to our downfall, through Amma's grace, this man's weakness for food brought him to spirituality. Of course, that does not mean that we should all concentrate only on eating our favorite foods and wait for God to appear before us.

God has given us intelligence and discrimination only to help us escape from the same fate as the animals in Shankaracharya's example. If we don't use these faculties properly, the sense organs will become a curse for us. In the *Dhammapada*, the Buddha says,

> *The rain could turn to gold and still your thirst would not be slaked.*
> *Desire is unquenchable—or it ends in tears, even in heaven.*

For most people today, the sense organs end up taking them away from God and causing a lot of suffering. However, we can turn the same sense organs into a blessing if we use them properly. Those who take an interest in spirituality strive to properly apply their intelligence and discrimination with respect to the sense objects, which takes them closer to God and removes their suffering.

Of course, we all know from experience that it is not easy to have perfect discrimination in using the sense organs. This is because our inherent tendencies, or vasanas, constantly delude us into believing that without certain things we can never be happy.

A man walks into a bar, orders three separate glasses of whiskey at the same time, and drinks all three. He does this for several days in a row. Finally the bartender says, "You know, I can put all three glasses in one big mug, if you want."

But the man says, "No, I prefer it this way. See, I have two brothers. This one is for my older brother; this one is for my younger brother, and the third one is for me. This way I can imagine we are all here having a glass of whiskey together."

The man continues to come in day after day, and the bartender always serves the whiskey in three glasses. Then one day the man says, "Give me just two glasses today."

Concerned, the bartender inquires, "Did something happen to one of your brothers?"

"No, no," the man replies. "They're both fine. It's just that I decided to quit drinking."

Like this, our mind will use twisted logic to justify our unnecessary desires. Even desires that are common to almost all of us, like getting married and having children, can lead us into trouble if we do not use our discrimination when fulfilling them. We should always move forward with caution without expecting too much, and above all we should listen to the advice of our Guru.

Once during one of Amma's foreign tours a young but very successful businessman told Amma that he had recently met and fallen in love with a young lady and was planning to marry her soon. Amma advised him, "Don't be in a hurry. Think about it for a while before you make your decision."

The next year the young man came for darshan again, this time with a lady at his side. Amma asked him, "Oh, did you get married?"

The young man replied, "Yes, Amma, she was so irresistible to me that I could not follow your advice. We got married a week after I saw you last."

The next time Amma returned to this city, the same young man came to see Amma. It had been three years since Amma had advised him to consider his decision before getting married. This time, the young man was alone, and he did not look so young anymore. Actually, he looked quite despondent and worn out. He told Amma that his wife had left him and had won half his wealth in divorce court; he had spent most of the remaining half in legal fees. He remorsefully told Amma that he really wished he had listened to Her advice. For this young man, the very same lady who he thought would give him everlasting happiness became the cause of what he was sure would be his everlasting sorrow.

There is another story about a couple in India who couldn't conceive a child after their marriage. Whenever they came to see Amma, they would tell Her that they wanted a child. Amma told them, "In your case, it is better not to have a child. Even if you have a child, I don't think the child will live very long." A True Master like Amma sees the past, present, and future of every one of us. Amma could see that due to their *prarabdha* (karma), this couple was destined to have a child who would die young. In trying to dissuade them from the decision to have a child, Amma was trying to spare them from having to undergo this painful experience.

However, this couple was so intent on having a baby that they were deaf to Amma's words of wisdom. Finally they issued Her an ultimatum: "Amma, if you don't give us a child, we will kill ourselves. Without a child of our own, we don't want to go on living."

Amma warned them again of the danger that lay ahead, but they were adamant. Finally Amma agreed to bless them with a child. Two years later the woman gave birth, but true to Amma's words, the child fell ill at the age of six and died soon after.

Even though Amma had warned them repeatedly, the child's death was a terrible shock for the couple. They sank into a depression and had to be admitted to a mental hospital. Now, with Amma's grace, they have almost recovered from the shock.

Modern society tells us that the fulfillment of desires is the ultimate aim of life, and we can measure our success to the extent that we have fulfilled our life's aims and ambitions. But the scriptures tell us that there is more to life than this, that at some point we will have to give up everything and focus our whole attention on the spiritual path. When a Master like Amma tells us clearly that something we desire is not going to be good for us, we should sincerely try to give up that attachment or those desires. Mahatmas do not speak empty words. While we feel that not getting what we want is a major tragedy, actually getting what we want may lead to an even bigger tragedy.

This is not to say that the desire to get married or to have a child is bad. There is nothing wrong in getting married, having children or pursuing worldly goals. These things are not in any way forbidden. The scriptures approve of getting married and having children as an essential stage in almost everyone's life. Approached in the right way, the householder's life, or family life, is an opportunity to exhaust our desires and vasanas, but we should remember that the desires cannot be exhausted completely unless we use our discrimination. We should never overlook the obvious; none of what we now call our own is going to remain with us forever.

In the *Bhagavad Gita*, Lord Krishna says,

dharmāviruddho bhūteṣu kāmo 'smi bharata ṛṣabha

*Whatever desire is not opposed to dharma; I am that
desire.*

(VII.11)

The scriptures never ask us to suppress our desires and vasanas
but, instead, to overcome them using our intellect, through logic
and reasoning. If we step back and analyze what we desire, we will
be able to see that there are limitations to the amount of happiness we can derive from anything that is impermanent. When
this becomes our firm conviction, the desires will slowly begin
to fall away of their own accord. If we suppress our desires and
force ourselves to conform to an unrealistically rigid discipline,
we might spend some years in an ashram but then come out and
want to get married. Before coming to an ashram, before taking
up a life of *brahmacharya* (celibacy and control of the senses in
general), we must intellectually convince ourselves that we don't
want the pleasures of the world, understanding that they are
never going to be able to give us permanent happiness. When
we use this type of discrimination, there is nothing to suppress;
we simply choose a different path.

Once two hunters went on an expedition in the remote wil-
derness, which was accessible only by airplane. They chartered a
plane loaded with provisions into the isolated region and asked
the pilot to return after two weeks. When the pilot returned, he
was surprised to find the hunters waiting with three huge buffaloes that they had bagged.

"Okay, we're ready to go," they told the pilot.

The pilot replied, "Just what do you think you are going to
do with those buffaloes?"

"Take them with us, of course. Do you think we're going to leave them behind?"

The pilot laughed and said, "There is no way that those three buffaloes are going to fit in our little plane. You're going to have to limit it to just one."

"Aww, c'mon!" whined the hunters. "Last year the pilot let us take three!"

The pilot was astonished. "Really?" he asked. "Well, I guess if you did it last year we can do it again this year. Let's give it a shot."

So, they somehow wedged two of the buffaloes inside the plane, tied another one on top of the plane's tail, and they were ready to go. With great difficulty, the pilot managed to take off and was struggling to gain altitude. But when a high ridge came up, they couldn't make it over, and the plane slammed into the side of the mountain. Fortunately, there were no fatalities.

Emerging from the wreckage, the pilot said, "Oh, great. Now where are we?"

The hunters were looking around very carefully, checking a compass, observing certain landmarks and comparing it against their map.

"Yep, yep, I think I know where we are," one of the hunters told the pilot confidently, looking up from the map. "Should be just about two miles east of where we crashed last year."

The buffaloes are our attachments and the airplane is the reality of life. Like the hunters, we go on and on attached to the objects of the world, repeating the same mistakes, then "crashing and burning," when we discover that the strength of our attachment to an object is disproportionate to the capacity of the object to give us happiness.

On the subject of buffaloes and desires, a devotee in the United States told me about a friend who loves to eat "buffalo wings" (tiny chicken wings). Whenever he gets the opportunity, he will eat as many as possible. But the next day, without fail, he feels terribly sick to his stomach, even to the extent of rolling around on the floor in pain. Even though he knows this will happen, he is not able to refrain from gorging himself on buffalo wings again and again.

Only human beings behave in such an illogical fashion. Hearing this story, I was reminded of the behavior of a particular kind of goat in India. The goat wanders here and there in search of vegetation to eat. Some leaves are very sticky. If the goat eats these leaves, they will get stuck in his throat, and he can choke and even die. But if one goat eats such a leaf, seeing its condition, all the other goats will avoid this leaf, not just on that day but from then on.

If peace could be found in external objects, wouldn't the wealthiest and most successful among us have found it long ago? In Her address at the 2004 Parliament of World's Religions in Barcelona, Amma said that the only difference between people in wealthy countries and people in poor countries is that the poor are crying on the dirt floors of their huts, while the rich are crying in air-conditioned rooms in palatial mansions. Any number of achievements or possessions does not seem to give us what we really want. As the Greek philosopher Plato put it, "Poverty is not the absence of goods, but rather the overabundance of desire." We are all looking for peace and happiness in objects and situations that are not capable of giving them to us.

The process of indulging the senses can be compared to a staircase leading downward. The first step is our attachment to a person or object; the next step down is in desiring to possess that object. The anger we experience when our desire is blocked is one more step, and when we are overcome by anger, we lose our discrimination and can easily tumble down the remaining steps into delusion and despair.

We should not think, however, that there is no hope for us. There is another staircase before us, and this one leads upward, away from attachment and suffering and into Liberation and everlasting bliss. The first step of this staircase leading upward is association with a True Master like Amma. The more time we spend in the company of a Master, the more we get attached to the Master's blissful presence. Becoming more attached to a Master automatically weakens our attachments to other people and the objects of the world.

In the Master's presence, we learn that we can experience peace, contentment and fulfillment without the help of any external objects. Thus, our tendency to pursue those objects is weakened. This relative lack of desire makes our mind less agitated and more peaceful. This peace gradually deepens within until we reach the top of the staircase leading upward to Liberation. In a world where most people are in a downward spiral, our attachment to the Master leads us upward—step by step—into freedom from all attachment and its attendant suffering.

Chapter 8

The Jewel of Discrimination

Once a journalist asked Amma, "From Amma's point of view, what is the most significant thing to keep in mind in daily life for the ordinary people of the world?" Amma replied, "The most important thing we must keep in mind is that while doing work in this world, we should always try to have a discriminative intellect, not just an intellect. To know what is Truth and what is untruth, what is good and what is bad—with that attitude, try to discharge your duties in the world."

When Amma says "discrimination," She does not mean "discriminatory," as in racial discrimination, nor "discriminating," as in the refined comparative sensibility of a connoisseur. In *Viveka Chudamani*, Shankaracharya defines *viveka*, or discrimination, as "the firm conviction that Brahman alone is eternal. Everything else is impermanent. This conviction is the discrimination between the Eternal and the ephemeral."

Thus, when Amma says, "Truth and untruth," She is not talking about understanding that someone is telling a lie. By Truth, She is referring to that which exists unchanged in the three periods of time—past, present and future. That which is, was and always will be is only the Self, or Atman. By untruth, Amma means all that is changing or perishable—in short, everything we see in the world around us. When Amma says "good and bad," good means any thought, word or action that will lead us closer to our goal of realizing our oneness with God, and bad means any thought, word or action that will take us further away from this goal. It is this sense of discrimination that differentiates us from the lower levels of life. How we use this discrimination determines the blessedness of our life.

We might read about the richest people in the world and aspire to be among their ranks. But we forget that our inborn quality of discrimination is worth more than all the money in the world. Using our faculty of discrimination and sense of dharma, we can become one with the infinite Atman.

If we do not use our discrimination in the right way, we waste the opportunity that is given to us in a human birth. This key of discrimination is in our hands; nobody is hiding it from us. Whether or not we unlock the door of our potential is entirely up to us. This decision lies in how we approach each situation in life and how we make use of the time that is given to us. Amma says that even if we lose a million dollars, we can get it back, but if we waste even a second, it is lost forever.

There is a famous Vedantic story that shows how we fail to use our discrimination in the proper way. A man was wandering through a forest when he happened upon several tiger cubs. When the mother tiger saw him standing there, she charged toward him. The man fled as fast as he could. In his haste, he fell into a deep well. As he fell, he was able to catch hold of a root growing out of the side of the well and stop his fall. Unfortunately, he noticed that a couple of mice were gnawing away at the root and that it would soon break away from the wall of the well. Even worse, debris falling from the side of the well had disturbed a large, menacing python that had been coiled at the bottom of the well and was now waiting patiently for him to plummet into its gaping maw. He thought he might have been able to climb back up to the top of the well, but when he looked up, he saw the angry tiger waiting to devour him as soon he was within reach.

As the man continued to take in his surroundings, he observed that in his fall he had broken off part of a beehive, which was now dripping fresh honey just above his head. When he saw that, he completely forgot all the dangers surrounding him and stuck out his tongue to try to catch a few drops of honey.

We may be shaking our head at his foolishness, but our situation is not so different. Instead of putting forth effort to save himself, the man, who was surrounded by danger on every side, was lost in the pursuit of the fleeting pleasure of the honey. Similarly, we are surrounded on all sides by dangers like sorrow, disease, old age and death, and yet we do not make any effort to transcend our limitations and break free from the cycle of birth and death. This shows that we are not using our discrimination properly.

Amma says that at present, most of us are walking around in a half-asleep state. She gives the example of a drunkard who returns home after a long night. When he looks in the mirror, he sees that his face is covered in scratches and wounds. Before going to bed, he carefully washes and bandages each scrape. In the morning, his wife finds the mirror covered in bandages.

Though we are physically awake, our level of wakefulness or awareness is usually very low. How often do we really concentrate on what we are doing? While we are eating breakfast, we are also reading the newspaper. While talking on the phone, we are doing the dishes. While reading a story to our children, we are thinking about our problems at work. And when we get to work, we are worrying about how our children are doing at school. With the advent of new technology, our concentration has become even more scattered. Even while visiting a temple, people do not hesitate to receive a call on their cell phone.

This low level of awareness is the reason we find ourselves repeating the same mistakes day after day. Each night we might regret having lost our temper and resolve never to do it again. But as soon as we feel someone has crossed us, we blow our top once more. If we were really alert and aware, we would remember our resolve to be patient and stick to it. Likewise, there are so many different diets available, and most people profess to adhere to one or another, but statistics show that very few really stick to their diet. The moment we lay eyes on a forbidden food, we forget all our dietary goals.

Amma points out that many people purchase a life-insurance policy to give some financial security to their near and dear ones. In taking the policy, they clearly indicate that they know their life is impermanent, but still everyone lives as if death were a very distant thing, something that will only come to others. In the great Indian epic *Mahabharata*, during their exile in the forest, four of the five Pandavas temporarily lose their lives by drinking water from a lake presided over by a *yaksha* (celestial being) who wanted to test Yudhishthira. In order to win back the lives of his brothers, Yudhishthira has to answer a set of riddles posed by the yaksha. At one point, the yaksha asks Yudhishthira, "What is the greatest wonder in the world?"

Yudhishthira answers the riddle to the demon's satisfaction. "Day after day countless lives enter into the Temple of Death. Looking on this spectacle, those who remain believe themselves to be permanent, immortal. Is there any greater wonder?"

Of course, many of us have never seen someone dying. Some of us might not have even seen a dead body. But we all hear about people dying every day in various parts of the world. In that way, death is very much a part of our daily life.

There is a story about a journalist who was interviewing a man on his 99th birthday. At the end of the interview, the journalist took the old man's hand and said earnestly, "I really hope I can come back to see you next year on your 100th birthday."

To this, the old man replied, "I don't see why not—you look healthy enough."

Just like the old man in the story, it rarely or never occurs to us that we, too, are going to die one day. Thus we don't feel any urgency to reach the goal of life.

Once during one of Amma's foreign tours, Amma and a small entourage were on a plane that encountered severe turbulence. We noticed with amusement that most of the passengers had been engrossed in the in-flight movie, but when the plane started to shake and drop suddenly, everyone became very devout, closing their eyes and praying with a great deal of concentration and devotion. However, as soon as the turbulence subsided, one by one those same passengers came back to their senses, as it were, and turned their attention back to the movie. One passenger even asked the flight attendant if the movie could be rewound to the place where it had been interrupted.

We may be quick to laugh at these travelers, but don't we all conduct our lives this way? Only when there is some threat, or some calamity befalls us, do we gain some detachment toward the objects of the world.

There were two childhood friends who grew up playing baseball together. They both played in amateur leagues throughout their lives until they were too old to even pick up a bat, and they followed the sport's professional teams with religious dedication. They were next-door-neighbors in the nursing home, and as they succumbed to old age and illness, they even agreed that whoever died first would try to come back and tell the other if there was baseball in heaven.

One summer night, one of the men passed away in his sleep after watching his favorite team come back to an unlikely victory earlier in the evening. A few nights later, the man who was still living woke to the sound of his old friend's voice from beyond.

"Is that you?" he asked the thin air, from where it sounded like his friend's voice was emanating.

"Of course it's me," the voice of his dead friend replied.

"This is unbelievable!" the living man exclaimed happily. "So tell me, is there baseball in heaven?"

"Well, I have some good news and some bad news," his dead friend told him. "Which do you want to hear first?"

"Tell me the good news first."

"Well, the good news is that yes, there is baseball in heaven."

"Oh, that's terrific! What could possibly be the bad news?"

"You're scheduled to pitch tomorrow night."

The truth is that one day death will come to us, and we will not be able to complete the movie, much less rewind it—we will have to leave it behind us. The only thing that will accompany us after death is the results of our actions, both good and bad. Recognizing this, we should not become angry with God, but rather hold on to Him even more tightly.

Amma often says that it is easy to wake someone who is sleeping but difficult to wake someone who is pretending to be asleep. The suggestion is that we are all pretending to be asleep. If we look at how we live, we will see that it is so.

Whenever we have to choose between what we know will benefit us spiritually and what is comfortable or easy, most of the time we choose what is more comfortable. Even psychologists say that generally speaking, their patients want relief rather than a real solution to their problems; to really solve their problems they would have to change their way of acting and responding to the world.

Some people argue that since everything in the world has been created by God, there is no such thing as good or bad, and we should feel free to do whatever we like. If we examine this argument closely, we can easily see its flaws. For example, many animals can survive only by preying on other animals. Intoxicating drugs are found in the natural kingdom. Does that then mean it's only natural to take drugs and commit murder?

Likewise, God created healthy fruits as well as poisonous fruits. Will we consume the poisonous berries as quickly as strawberries, saying they are only natural? Yet, when we make a less than noble decision, we often justify our behavior by saying, "It's only natural."

That may be true, but spirituality does not consist of acting natural. In fact, it consists of transcending our lower, animalistic nature. It has been said that we are not human beings who have spiritual experiences, but spiritual beings who have the experience of being human.

In the early days of the ashram, Amma insisted that all of the ashramites get up at 4:00 a.m., regardless of what time they went to sleep. Thus, usually all the lights in the ashram were out by 11:00 p.m. On one such evening, Amma called me to Her room at about 10:30 p.m. When I got there, She was talking with a family, so I waited outside. But by 11:00 p.m., the family still had not left. Though I knew the right thing to do was to obey Amma's instructions, I also knew I would have to get up at 4:00 a.m. no matter how late I was up waiting to meet with Amma. So, a few minutes after 11:00 p.m., I went back to my hut to sleep. When I opened my eyes, it was not 4:00 but 7:00 a.m.

Later, I found out that around midnight Amma asked someone to see if I was still waiting there, but when She was informed that I was gone, She did not ask for me again, saying, "Let him sleep." By ignoring what I knew was right, I missed both the opportunity to be with Amma and the next day's morning prayers, too.

This story illustrates an important point: When we pretend to be asleep, there is a great danger that we will actually fall asleep. When we indulge in something, even though we might remember at first that true happiness does not lie in the object, before long we may be completely caught up in it, forgetting all about God and the real goal of life.

We should be courageous. Let us not bury ourselves deeper in the sleeping bag of ignorance. Instead, let us accept the reality that we will never get true contentment from the world and that spirituality is the only solution. Let us rise up and embrace the supreme dharma, moving forward with discrimination.

Chapter 9

The Secret of Success

Amma says, "We all receive education for livelihood, but not education for life." Spirituality is this education for life, and it is the real foundation of life. If we build this foundation at a young age through understanding spiritual principles, we won't stumble and fall when faced with the trials of life. One of the cornerstones of spiritual life is self-discipline. No one wants to hear about self-discipline, but those who don't have it eventually discover how important it is. Even those who manage to climb high on the ladder of name, fame, power and wealth eventually crumble in front of trivial pleasures and temptations, resulting in defamation and agony. Perhaps this is what prompted the late American actress Katherine Hepburn to quip, "Without discipline, there's no life at all."

In order to make real spiritual progress, self-discipline is essential. Self-discipline is not about punishment or even about a restrictive lifestyle. It is the ability of the individual to adhere to actions, thoughts and behaviors that result in personal improvement instead of instant gratification. A lack of self-discipline is the main reason for the failures we experience in both our personal and professional lives.

Once a woman walked up to a frail, wrinkled man with stringy gray hair, rocking back and forth in a chair on his porch.

"Excuse me sir," she said, "but I just couldn't help noticing how happy you look. What's your secret for a long happy life?"

"Well, my child," the man answered with a toothless grin, "I smoke three packs of cigarettes a day, drink a case of whiskey a week, eat fatty foods, listen to heavy-metal music, and never exercise."

"That's amazing!" she said, "I've never heard of such a secret for longevity! How old are you?"

"Twenty-six," he said.

Self-discipline is much like the operating systems we use for our computers. A computer without an operating system is much like a person who lacks discipline. They both have a tremendous amount of potential and power but have no way of functioning properly. Unlike a computer, we are blessed with the gift of free will, but without self-discipline we are susceptible to the viruses of instant gratification, excuses and bad habits.

The Greek philosopher Aristotle said, "I count him braver who overcomes his desires than him who conquers his enemies, for the hardest victory is over self." It is not always easy to comprehend the benefit of maintaining a disciplined life, as it so often seems more enjoyable, profitable and convenient to do otherwise.

From the very earliest days of the ashram, it was part of our discipline to wake up at 4:00 a.m., have a bath and gather together to chant the 1000 Names of the Divine Mother. One day soon after I joined the ashram, I woke up at 4:00 a.m. and found that it was quite cold, as it had rained all throughout the previous day. As there was only cold water available, I decided to skip the bath and go straight to the morning archana. I figured I could wait until the air warmed up before having a bath. The rain continued that day and for several more, and I continued my new practice of going to archana without bathing first. After a few days, when I stepped outside to go to the *kalari*[5] for the archana, I found a large bucket of steaming hot water next to the door of my hut. I was surprised, but I didn't want to waste the opportunity; I immediately took it to the bathroom and had my shower. Later, I asked the other brahmacharis to find out who was the good Samaritan who had heated the water for me. None of them knew anything about it. When I saw Amma that afternoon, She casually asked me, "Did you have a nice bath this morning?" With that I had no doubt about who had placed the hot water there for me. I was pained at the thought of Amma laboring to heat water over a smoking wood fire just so I would be willing to follow the ashram discipline of bathing before worship. I realized then that a Guru will go to any extent to correct the disciple, and after that I never missed my morning bath no matter how cold it might have been.

Of course, we cannot take advantage of Amma's humility and patience to make our own lives easier. If I had simply waited for Amma to bring me a bucket of hot water every morning, I am sure She would have quickly changed tactics. In fact, some years later, when many more brahmacharis had joined the ashram, there were a few who developed a habit of sleeping through the archana in spite of Amma's repeated reminders. Finally, Amma had to resort to drastic measures. One morning She entered the hall where they were sleeping and splashed cold water over all of them. About this, Amma later said, "All of you have come here

---

[5] In Sanatana Dharma, kalari means any place of worship where there is no deity installed. This was the name given to the ashram's original temple, which was not much bigger than a walk-in closet and had been converted from Amma's family's cowshed. Looking back, it is amazing to consider that Amma, who now often gives programs in amphitheaters and stadiums, could ever have given darshan in such a small space.

with the intention of realizing God. Thus, it has become Amma's duty to make you aware of your mistakes and help you overcome them. If you are lazy even in small matters, how can you attain Liberation?"

Over the years, the number of people coming to see Amma at Amritapuri (and around the world) has continued to increase, and She finishes the darshan later and later. Finally, about two years ago, the "morning" darshan began extending even past 6:30 p.m., which is the time Amma used to come for the evening bhajans. When Amma had to give darshan until 7:00 p.m. or even 8:00 p.m., of course She could not come for the bhajans. Still, the swamis would come to sing and all the brahmacharis and ashram residents, except those directly involved in helping with the darshan line, were expected to attend. However, on the days when Amma was giving darshan through the evening bha-jans, some brahmacharis would not attend, instead doing some other work or sitting alone in meditation. One evening, Amma finished giving darshan just before 7:00 p.m. Since it was already late, many people thought Amma would not go for bhajans and they also went their own way. However, when Amma came down the spiral stairs from the darshan hall, She did not turn right and head up to Her room as everyone expected but turned left and headed straight for the bhajan hall. She did not even take time to change Her clothes or wash Her face. As many brahmacharis did not expect Amma to be there for the bhajans, they did not attend. Only after hearing Amma's voice over the loudspeakers did they realize that She was there, and they all came running. Seeing Amma sitting on the stage with Her hair out of place and Her sari stained by the tears and makeup of the thousands of devotees whom She had embraced that day was a heartbreaking sight for everyone, and they quickly learned the lesson Amma was trying to impart to them. If She could stick to the ashram discipline even after such a rigorous darshan, who could excuse themselves from doing the same? Now, even if Amma has to give darshan late into the night, all the brahmacharis go for the evening bhajans. And yet, Amma still does everything She can to attend the bhajans Herself. She has even started coming out an hour earlier for the morning darshan, and whenever She is finished, She goes straight to the bhajan hall.

Success in life comes when we do not succumb to what we want to do, but rise to undertake what ought to be done. Most of us only want to do what we like. In order to progress spiritually, we must learn to like what we have to do. To arrive at this point, we can begin with the commitment to do what needs to be done, whether we like it or not. If we discipline ourselves in this way, naturally we will begin to like doing what is required in any given situation—not doing what we like, but liking what we are called upon to do.

We cannot live our lives by emotions alone; to achieve any goal at all, we need to add discipline. Just as external discipline makes things go smoothly in the outside world, internal discipline helps to create order in our mind, which can then be directed toward the ultimate goal of Self-realization.

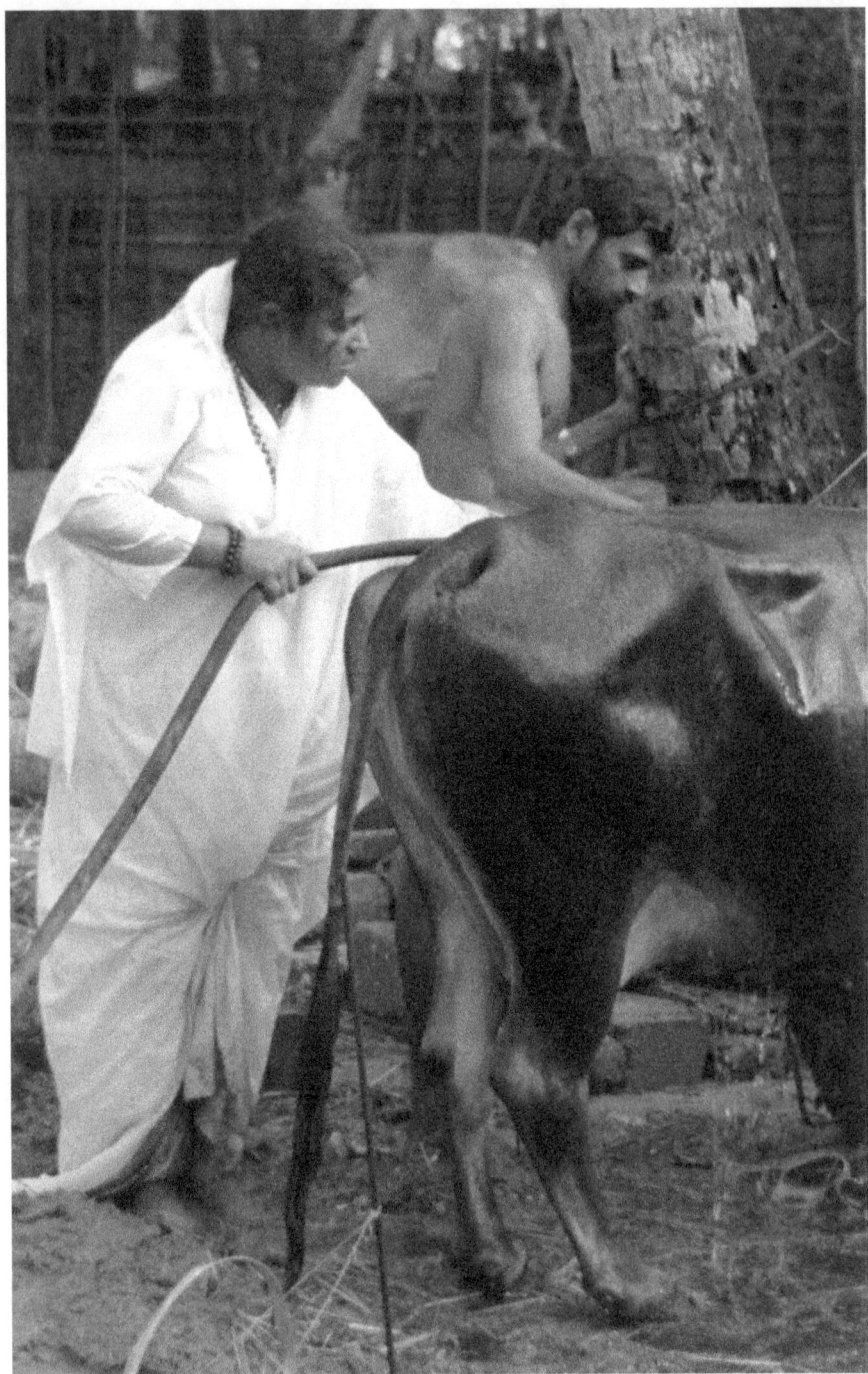

Chapter 10

Action, Experience and Beyond

Amma says our day-to-day life is composed of two primary elements: action and experience. If we know how to act in the right way and how to approach our experiences, our life can be relatively peaceful.

To act in the right way means to act without being attached to the result. In the *Bhagavad Gita*, Lord Krishna declares, *yogah karmasu kausalam*, which means "Skill in action is yoga." Here, Krishna does not mean simply that we should be good at doing a particular task. In that case, every skilled tradesman would be a yogi. What Krishna really means by skill in action is maintaining equanimity of mind, irrespective of the result of the actions we perform. Of course, this doesn't mean that we don't need any talent or skill. For instance, there are those who do not study well for an exam and are not at all bothered when they fail. This cannot be called yoga. Putting forth our best effort without worrying or feeling anxious about the result of our action is called yoga. To work sincerely without allowing our mind to move away from the present moment is skill in action. This is what is meant by, "performing action for action's sake."

Of course, if we take an examination, we all hope and expect to pass, and we will not go for a job interview if we don't expect to be hired. Without any expectations at all, we might lose our motivation to perform even good actions. So rather than not expecting any result, we can expect all results. That is, we can expect to be hired, but we should expect not to be hired as well.

We may think it is easier to refrain from performing actions at all. But as human beings, the truth is that we are always in action, from the moment of birth until the moment of death. One of Amma's devotees used to boast about his habit of sleeping 12 hours or more each night. He considered it a service to humanity. "At least at that time I am not harming anyone," he told me. But the truth is that we cannot possibly avoid action; it is part of the nature of being alive. Even when we are asleep, our body is performing involuntary action at the physiological level—our heart is beating, our lungs are taking air and our blood is circulating oxygen and nutrients throughout our body.

In the *Bhagavad Gita*, Lord Krishna says,

> na hi kaścit kṣaṇam api jātu tiṣṭhaty akarmakṛt
> kāryate hy avaśaḥ karma sarvaḥ prakṛtijair guṇaiḥ

None can ever remain really inactive even for a moment; for everyone is helplessly driven to action by the qualities of their innate nature.

(III.5)

In addition to physical actions and physiological actions, we are performing actions at the mental level as well; even thinking is a kind of action. Though we might manage to sit still, our mind races from past to future and back again. As long as we are identified with the body, mind and intellect, we are bound by the laws of nature and helplessly driven to action. Accepting this fact, it is worth understanding how to act in the right way.

For example, some people buy a lottery ticket once a week. Even if they don't win the lottery, they're not upset; they keep trying. Of course, I don't mean to say that we should buy lottery tickets. It's just an example to show that even if we don't succeed in our efforts to achieve a particular result, we shouldn't become frustrated or depressed. As long as there is a good possibility of success, we should keep trying. If we sincerely put forth effort and after repeated attempts still do not succeed, we have to accept it in a positive light.

This brings us to the other primary element in leading a peaceful life: approaching our experiences in the right way so that our each and every experience helps us to grow spiritually and does not disturb our equanimity. Amma says there are several ways we can do this.

A devotee will try to see all experiences, both positive and negative, as coming from God or coming from the Guru. In doing so, we are not lying to ourselves. Even though it is the result of our karma, the law of karma is functioning only because of God. So indirectly, it is coming from God. Even those who don't have faith in God or spiritual laws believe that in the long run, if we do a good thing we will get a good result, and if we do a bad thing we will get a bad result. Everyone agrees that the result may not come immediately; the only difference between this common-sense understanding and the spiritual perspective is that according to the law of karma, the result may not even come in this lifetime. That is why we can see some people who suffer so much while they do not seem to have done anything wrong in their entire life, while there are those who perform only harmful actions and seemingly prosper. In this case, the only explanation is that each one is experiencing the results of actions he or she performed in a past life. Later on, either in this life or the next, that person will have to experience the results of the actions he or she is performing now, whether enjoyable or painful.

A man is sitting down to read the paper when he hears a knock on his door. Upon opening the door, the man is confronted by a snail on his doorstep. "Good evening," says the snail. "I'm collecting for the Snail Benevolent Fund. Would you care to make a donation?" The snail gets his reply as a kick into the bushes.

Two weeks later there's another knock at the door. Again, the man finds a snail on his doorstep. "That wasn't very nice!" exclaims the snail.

Whatever happens to us is our own prarabdha, or the results of our past actions that we are due to experience in this life. We all know the expression, "Don't kill the messenger." This expression has its origins in warfare, when one side would send an unarmed person to deliver a message to the enemy. It was commonly understood that the messenger should not be punished even if delivering unfavorable news; the messenger is only doing his duty. We can take a similar attitude toward those who mistreat us, seeing someone who criticizes or abuses us as no more than a messenger delivering to us the results of our own past actions. It is the law of the universe that if we have not done anything to deserve misfortune in this life or a previous one, no misfortune will befall us. Therefore, there is no point in getting angry with someone who mistreats us; in fact, we can even feel grateful to him or her for helping us to exhaust our remaining prarabdha.

At the same time, we should remember that in any painful or unpleasant experience, there is always something for us to learn. Even if we are unfairly blamed for something, we can learn from our reaction. We can use the situation as an opportunity to develop more kindness, patience and love.

Many years back, I was standing some distance from where Amma was giving darshan, and I got into an argument with a devotee. I can no longer recall the subject of the argument, but I remember that suddenly Amma interrupted me and called me over to Her. When I went near Amma, She told me, "Your face looks like an *ondu* (a type of Kerala garden lizard renowned for being particularly ugly)."

When Amma said this, I was quite taken aback. "After all," I thought, "many people have told me I am handsome. Why is Amma saying the opposite?"

Over the next few days, Amma called me several more times and told me the same thing. Though I was upset, I did not react outwardly but just accepted Amma's words. The third time She said it to me, suddenly an incident from my past flashed before my eyes. It had happened many years earlier, before I had met Amma, when I was still in college. At that time I had a friend who had slightly peculiar looks. One day, out of the blue, I told him, "Hey, your face looks like a rat." I said it casually, without thinking, but my friend took it very seriously. After that he did not talk to me for several days, and sometimes when I saw him I could tell that he had been crying.

Finally he approached me and said, "Ramakrishna, what you said really hurt me. I have never felt so bad in my life as I felt when you said that." I told him I was sorry, but things were never quite the same between us, and it was clear that he was deeply pained by what I had said to him.

It is said that making an innocent person cry is one of the surest ways to block the flow of God's grace from reaching us. Remembering that incident, I understood that this was Amma's way of exhausting any negative karma I had incurred by speaking those words so long ago. After that I was able to accept Amma's words without even a ripple of negativity in my heart.

Those who have faith in God always think that God is the dispenser of the results of our actions. As far as a real seeker or a perfect devotee is concerned, there is no such thing as pain or pleasure—everything is a gift from God, or a blessing from the Guru.

There is a story about a famous rabbi named Zushia who lived about 200 years ago. Rabbi Zushia was widely revered for leading a pious, simple and devout life. In a town near where Rabbi Zushia lived, there was a rabbinical college. The students were studying the *Talmud* and came to the passage that says: "We must thank God for the good as well as the bad." The students were puzzled. Thanking God for the good, that's understandable and reasonable, but thanking God for the bad? That didn't make any sense.

They brought this question to the attention of the dean of the college. He stroked his long beard and pondered the question. "This is a question that only Rabbi Zushia can answer. Go to his house and ask him!"

Rabbi Zushia lived in a secluded area outside of the town. The students walked beyond the town's limits and entered the wooded forest. Following a narrow path, they soon arrived at a run-down shack that was the rabbi's abode. The windows were broken, the roof looked in need of repair and the walls were badly cracked. As Rabbi Zushia greeted them and led them in, they saw the abject poverty in which he lived. The chairs were wobbly and few. The other furnishings were shoddy and in poor repair.

The rabbi apologized for not having anything to offer them to eat and asked if perhaps a glass of hot water would be sufficient.

The students explained that they had come to ask him this question: "Why does it say in the *Talmud* that we must thank God for the good as well as the bad?"

"Why should you come to me to ask that question?" Rabbi Zushia countered. "I cannot understand it either. Nothing bad has ever happened to me. Is it possible that God does anything bad?"

A devotee always has the faith that God knows exactly what he or she needs and will always provide for him or her. Even bitter experiences are accepted as for his or her own good, the same way one willingly drinks bitter medicine when one knows it will cure a disease.

From the point of view of Vedanta, the highest spiritual philosophy of Sanatana Dharma, there is another state beyond acting and experiencing called *sakshi bhava*, or the witness state. In the witness state, not only do we not identify with the results of our actions, we do not identify with the actions themselves. Whatever we do is a spontaneous response to the circumstances that present themselves to us. We will do whatever is needed in a given situation, but in this state, we remain as a witness to both our actions and our experiences. We are identified only with the Atman, the Pure Consciousness that illuminates all of life.

At present, of course, we are not able to do that. When we are hungry, or when we are eating or when we are in pain, we are identified with the body. When we are feeling angry or sad, we are identified with the mind. And whenever we make a decision of any kind, we are identified with the intellect.

The door to the witness state is right in front of us; it is hiding in these very day-to-day activities that absorb much of our energy and attention.

When we are hungry, we know, "I am hungry." When we are angry, we know, "I am angry." And when we are confused, we know, "I'm confused." That means that the body, the mind and the intellect are all objects of our observation. For every object of observation, there must be a subject that is aware of the object. This awareness, the eternal subject, is our *Atman*, our True Self. Identifying with this state is the true sakshi bhava.

We think of the awareness within ourselves as being a separate awareness from the awareness in the person next to us. But the ancient Sages looked deep within and found that this subjective awareness does not belong to anyone in particular—it is the same in all beings.

Amma points out that even in our day-to-day life, we encounter this great truth. Whenever we introduce ourselves, we say, "I am John" or "I am Lakshmi." And we might also tell someone, "I am a Christian" or "I am a Jew," "I am a lawyer," "I am a monk," etc. In all these apparent differences, we can see that the "I am" is common. That "I" is not different in different people, but is the same Self that is present as the awareness in all beings. Amma gives the example of watching a funeral procession passing by. When the person was alive, we would have said, "There goes Peter," but now that the person is dead, we don't say that. Instead we say, "There goes Peter's body." This means that Peter is not the body but something beyond. Even when someone is alive, we talk in a similar fashion. We might say, "His body is very strong" or "His mind is weak." Also: "She has a very sharp intellect." But we never stop to think, who is that he or that she to which we refer?

Whether we know it or not, we recognize that there is something beyond the body, mind and intellect all the time. But we are unable to incorporate this fact into our direct experience.

In this regard Amma tells the following story. A lady loses her son in a car accident, and she is understandably distraught.

Her neighbor consoles her by referring to the scriptures and the teachings of the Realized Masters, telling her, "You are not the body, you are the Atman. The Atman is all-pervading and is never born and never dies. Therefore, where could your son go?"

The grieving mother gains a great deal of strength from her neighbor's advice. A month later, the neighbor's husband is killed in an accident at work. At that time, the woman who lost her son the previous month tries to console her neighbor with the same spiritual wisdom that the neighbor had given her the month before. But now, the neighbor is inconsolable. The woman says, "Just last month you told me all of these spiritual truths! Why don't you listen to them now?"

"That was when *your* son died," the woman explained. "But now we are talking about *my* husband!"

Like this, it is easy to be a witness toward the experience of others, but when it is our own experience, it is another story.

Once, a pundit was teaching classes on Vedanta in a forest ashram. The pundit was telling the students over and over, "Only the Atman, the Self, is eternal—all else is *maya* (illusion). Never fall into the trap of maya." Suddenly, a huge bull elephant with long, sharp tusks came charging wildly from the forest toward the ashram. As the pundit was sitting on a platform facing the forest, he was the first to see the elephant approaching. He was also the first to start running. Seeing the pundit run, all the students also got up and ran after him. After fleeing to safety, one of the disciples said, "Punditji, I never knew you could run so fast! By the way, you were saying that everything is maya, but if everything is maya, then why did you run, seeing the elephant?"

Having already regained his composure, the pundit coolly replied, "It's true that the elephant is maya, but then my running away was also maya." The pundit was able to teach from his intellect, but under the pressure of circumstances he lacked the mental strength to be able to live the teaching.

Along similar lines, I read a true-life story about the making of a recent film on the last hours of the life of Christ. During the shooting of the film, the actor portraying Jesus was pretending to be scourged by stuntmen holding real leather whips, bearing the abuse with otherworldly patience and forbearance. By accident, one of the stuntmen actually struck the actor with the whip. Like any of us might do in a similar situation, the actor immediately cried out in pain and angrily cursed the stuntman.

It is easy to pretend that we are very patient and forgiving, but under trying circumstances we usually slip—or plunge head-long—back into our negative qualities of anger and impatience. Anyone can quote the scriptures and say, "I am the Supreme Consciousness," but who among us can put this into practice and manifest real divine qualities under all circumstances of life?

A person whose mind is completely pure is able to realize his or her true nature by merely listening to the words of the Master. For the vast majority of us, however, it is not enough for the Master to tell us, "You are the Supreme Being." This is because our true nature is veiled by layers of ignorance composed of our desires, attachments and our strong identification with our limited ego. Amma tells the following story.

Once a Guru sent two disciples to the market to purchase supplies for the ashram. When they returned, one of the disciples had obviously been roughed up, and the other one was red-faced and angry.

The Guru asked the disciples what had happened.

The first disciple said, "He beat me black and blue!"

The second disciple said, "Only because he called me a monkey!"

The Guru rebuked the second disciple, saying, "Though I have told you hundreds of times over the past so many years, 'You are not the body, the mind or the intellect, you are the Supreme Consciousness,' you never believed me. When your brother called you a monkey just once, you believed him."

Even though the disciple had been listening to the Guru's words and the scriptural statements, it had not gone deep into his heart.

Amma has demonstrated many times how a fully purified mind spontaneously responds to statements about the divine and experiences divinity then and there. When She was only 16 years old, She happened to pass by a reading of the *Srimad Bhagavatam* at a house in Her neighborhood. When the reader began to the recite the story of Lord Krishna's life, Amma spontaneously entered into a total identification with the Lord. Everyone at the house was irresistibly attracted to Her beautiful smile and enchanted mood. This was the beginning of Amma's Krishna Bhava darshan.

In the great Indian epic *Ramayana*, Hanuman needs to travel quickly to Lanka to bring a message to Sita, the beloved of his Lord Rama who is being held captive by the demon king Ravana. Actually, Hanuman is a god and has tremendous powers, but in his childhood he used to harass the *Rishis* (Seers) with various pranks and practical jokes, and they cursed him so that he would forget his powers. Later on, they blessed him saying that if someone reminds him of his powers, he would remember them and be able to use them. So, as Hanuman was standing on the seashore looking forlornly in the direction of Lanka, he was surrounded by Lord Rama's army of monkeys, who knew that Hanuman alone could leap to Lanka. As they started singing his praises, reminding him of his hidden powers, he immediately remembered his divine nature and rose to the occasion, crossing the sea and reaching Lanka in a single giant leap.

Like Hanuman, we have forgotten our divine nature. The many scriptural declarations such as, "Thou art That," are singing the praises of our True Self in order to remind us of who we really are.

To become established in the experience of oneness with the Supreme, the scriptures tell us we have to follow a three-step process—that of listening, reflection and contemplation. The first step is called *sravanam* (listening), which means listening to (or reading) the teachings of the scriptures and the Great Masters. We read in the scriptures and hear from the Masters that we are not the body, mind or intellect but, instead, the Atman that enlivens these three.

But because our minds are not pure, doubts arise when our Master's teachings contradict our daily experience. The Master says, "You are infinite Existence, Consciousness and Bliss." But our experience is that we are limited, sorrowful and subject to destruction. Therefore, the next step after sravanam is *mananam* (reflection), which is to reflect deeply on the Master's teaching. When the Master says to the wave in the ocean, "You are limitless," the wave has to first understand that as long as it identifies itself as a wave, it is limited, but when it realizes its true nature as the vast ocean itself, it becomes limitless.

Once Lord Rama asked Hanuman, "Who are you?"

Hanuman's reply beautifully illustrates the various perspectives from which we can approach the Supreme: "Oh Lord, when I think that I am this body, I am Your servant. When I think of myself as a *jiva* (individual soul), I am part of You. When I think of myself as the Atman, I am You. This is my conviction."

Hanuman knew that his relationship to the Lord depended on how broad a perspective he was able to take.

Through reflection we come to understand that we are not the limited body, mind and intellect, but the limitless Consciousness. When we have become intellectually convinced beyond a shadow of a doubt that this is the Truth, we have to assimilate this teaching so deeply that we transcend our mistaken identification with the body, mind and intellect and become completely identified with Consciousness. This process is called *nidhidhyasanam* or contemplation.

In contemplation, the disciple makes a habit of continuously thinking, in and through each and every action, each and every experience, "I am not the body or the mind—I am the pure Consciousness without beginning or end." Our response to any given situation, if one is called for, should be guided by that Truth. Through continuously maintaining thoughts of the Master's teachings and sincerely following the Master's instructions, the disciple becomes pure enough to realize the Truth. The Realized Master is like a matchbox, while the fully matured disciple is like a dry matchstick—a slight friction with the matchbox and it catches fire. However, only the grace and guidance of the Master can take the disciple to this fully matured state.

We cannot force sleep to come. We can lie down in a comfortable bed, make sure the room is dark and quiet, that we are warm enough, but when it comes to actually falling asleep, we have no choice but to wait patiently. Just as the urge to sleep chases away every other thought in the mind and drags the person to the bedroom, so too the constant contemplation on the Vedantic truth of nonduality chases away every other thought in the disciple's mind. However, it is only by the Guru's grace that the disciple is lifted into the highest state.

The Vedantic path, or realizing the Truth by direct study of and reflection on the Truth—which is without name or form—is extremely difficult. In fact, it is not suitable for most people. Even Adi Shankaracharya, who re-established the supremacy of the Advaita Vedanta philosophy of non-dualism, composed many hymns in praise of the Divine Mother because he knew that the path of Advaita was very difficult for most people to follow. The Buddha advocated an essentially nondualistic path and instructed his followers not to worship him or any form. And yet today, the largest religious statue in the world is of the Buddha. This shows that for the vast majority of people, worship of a formless God is difficult or impossible.

In the *Bhagavad Gita*, Lord Krishna says,

kleṣo 'dhikataras teṣām avyaktāsakta cetasām
avyaktā hi gatir duḥkhaṁ dehavadbhir avāpyate

Greater is their difficulty whose minds are set on the Unmanifested, for the goal of the Unmanifested is very hard for the embodied to reach.

(XII.5)

For most of us, it is enough if we can remember to act and experience in the right way. If we can act with the understanding that we are just an instrument in God's hands or remember that we have a right to act but not to determine the results of the actions, we can reach a state of equanimity toward our experiences that is very close to the witness state. On the path of devotion, too, we reach a place where we are not affected by good or bad, success and failure, happiness or sorrow. In surrendering to God's will, or the Guru's will, we still put forth effort and do our best to achieve our goals, but if we do not succeed, or if we meet with some misfortune, we accept it with an even mind and a peaceful heart. If our efforts meet with success, we accept that, too, as the grace of our Master.

When we visit a temple, we worship the deity therein, and the temple priest offers us some prasad. It might be payasam, fruit or nuts. Whatever it is, we accept it as a precious gift from the Lord. On the path of devotion, this dynamic is extended to apply to every aspect of our life. We see each of our actions as worship of our Guru, and we see the results of our actions as well as all other experiences that come to us, as the Guru's prasad. Thus we neither become elated in success nor depressed in failure. Rather, we are always content. This sense of equanimity stems from doing our best to surrender to God or the Guru. Through surrender, we let go of our ego, our sense of "I" and "mine," and see everything as God, or Guru, alone.

In one path, we see everything as God, and in the other, we see everything as the Self. Amma says that when we worship God with form, it will take us to a place from where it is very easy to realize the Supreme Self, and that for a true devotee who has reached the state of supreme devotion, God Himself will lead him or her to the realization of the nondual state.

Chapter 11

Putting the Horse Before the Cart – Understanding the Importance of Worship

In today's world, many people question the validity of deity worship or worship of a living Master. Sometimes people ask Amma, "Since form is ultimately an illusion, isn't Vedanta against worship of any particular form?" or, "If the Supreme Truth is without name or form, why should we meditate on a god with attributes like Ganesha, Shiva or Kali? Why should we meditate on a Guru?"

Anyone who picks up an advanced text like one of the Upanishads can frame seemingly intelligent questions like these, since the Upanishads praise contemplation on the formless Brahman as the highest form of spiritual practice. Those who are more intellectually inclined may be inspired by such texts and may even adopt contemplation on Brahman as their primary spiritual practice. But if they do so without proper guidance, they rarely make any real spiritual progress.

Of course, study of the scriptures is essential for any spiritual aspirant, but when we begin to approach the scriptures, we should be careful where we start. Nowadays, of course, many of the scriptures are easily available. They have been translated and published in many different languages and are even available on the internet. However, many English translations have been written without understanding the deeper meaning of what is said in the scriptures. For example, the Sanskrit word *pashu* means "animal." Thus some of the most popular translations say that the scriptures advocate the sacrifice of animals, while a more correct translation of exactly the same verse will say that the scriptures are telling us that we have to transcend our animalistic tendencies and experience our oneness with the Universal Self, the Atman.

Once the *devas* (celestial beings), the *asuras* (demons)and the human beings were all doing *tapas* (austerities). Suddenly they heard the sound, "da," reverberating through the air. They all took it as a message from God, but each one interpreted the message in a different way. Human beings thought "da" signified *danam*, or charity. They thought God was telling them to be more generous. Meanwhile, the asuras thought it meant *daya*, or compassion. And the devas thought the sound was telling them to exercise more *damam*, or restraint over the senses. Not surprisingly, the greatest flaw of human beings was selfishness, the asuras were cruel and hard-hearted, and the devas were ever indulging in the pleasures of the celestial realms. Each one imagined that God was telling them to cultivate a virtue corresponding to their respective weaknesses.

Similarly, one will interpret the scriptures according to his or her own level of understanding.

The scriptures have only been written down fairly recently. In the olden days, the scriptures were taught orally in a *gurukula* (traditional school). The Guru would recite the scriptures and the students were able to retain everything in their memory, and from memory they would teach their disciples. That is why another word for scripture in Sanskrit is *shruti*, or "that which came down though hearing." Because the students were able to hear it directly from the mouth of the Guru, there was no misunderstanding. Now it is all printed and anyone can read it and get confused. In fact we are already confused, and in reading advanced scriptures we only get more confused. Whatever clarity we did have will vanish if we read these scriptures without the guidance of a Realized Master.

It is good to start with the *Bhagavad Gita*, but even before beginning to read this famous text, Amma always recommends we cultivate the qualities of innocence, devotion and surrender to God. For that, we have to read the books of great devotees of God, devotees of the Lord who had these qualities in abundance. It is very important that we develop these qualities before we begin to study the scriptures, because the scriptures are going to tell us that we are the Supreme Self and everything else is an illusion. If we study the scriptures without first cultivating the requisite qualities, we will start thinking, "Why should I do spiritual practices, why should I go to a Master? I am the Truth, therefore I can do anything I want."

To illustrate the fallacy of this attitude, Amma gives the example of the seed and the tree. Of course, a huge, flowering tree can give shade, fruit and flowers to those who pass by. However, can the seed boast that it can offer such gifts to the world? Even though the tree is contained within the seed, it must first go beneath the soil, break open, take root, become a sapling, and slowly grow into a tree. Likewise, what is the use of ordinary people going around saying, "I am Brahman"? It has to become our experience.

We cannot become established in the experience of the Truth just by reading advanced texts, but at the same time, it is only through knowledge that we can attain Self-realization. All the meditation, seva and other spiritual practices we do are only to purify our mind; they cannot directly take us to Liberation. This is because the Self is not something that is newly created; the Self is already there. It is all-pervading and has always existed. In attaining Liberation, we are not actually gaining anything, but realizing the truth of what already is. That is why it is called Realization. For example, if we lose our glasses, we will search everywhere for them. But what happens when someone tells us that in fact we are already wearing our glasses? Did we then gain something we had lost? The glasses were there on our face all the time—we just had to realize it.

That is why it is said that we cannot realize the Self by doing something in particular such as chanting a fixed number of mantras or meditating for a certain period of time. Rather, just as the sun hidden by clouds is revealed as the clouds drift away, when our internal impurities, vasanas and the other mental disturbances are slowly removed through our spiritual practices and the grace of the Guru, real *jnana* (the knowledge that we are the Self) will dawn naturally and effortlessly within. When we become aware that "I am Brahman"—with the same degree of unshakeable certainty that we are now aware, "I am a human being"—this is Self-realization.

When I came to the ashram more than 27 years ago, the first book that Amma gave to me and the other brahmacharis to read was the life and teachings of Sri Ramakrishna Paramahamsa. When we read books about Great Masters who had so much devotion, humility and innocence, it helps to purify our heart. If someone is egoistic and proud, we are not impressed. But when we find someone who is truly humble, who is truly innocent, that way of being impresses us. Amma says that an innocent, simple heart is the key to making progress in spirituality: "One who is really in search of the Truth will have humility and simplicity. The Guru's grace will be showered only on such a person. To really live spiritually and attain real spiritual experience, one must develop the qualities of love, humility and innocence."

When we read the scriptures, we may come across descriptions of different spiritual practices. But these practices are not for everybody. Without the guidance of a True Master, it will be very difficult for us to know in what way we should practice. Amma gives the example of a very powerful tonic for increasing health, energy and vitality. The tonic is good for us, but if we drink the whole bottle thinking that we will derive more benefit, it will spoil our health. If we take it according to the prescribed dose, it will be very beneficial for us.

In 1987, during Amma's first world tour, one of the brahmacharis read the ingredients on a bottle of prune juice and saw that it was very rich in Vitamin C. As a doctor had recently advised him to take more Vitamin C, he decided to drink the whole bottle. At that time we had never left India and had never seen bottled juiced before. The brahmachari was very satisfied with his decision to drink the entire bottle and was telling the rest of us how much Vitamin C he had taken. Within a few hours, and for the next three days, he had such terrible diarrhea that he could not even come for Amma's programs.

If someone knowledgeable about prune juice had warned him not to take too much, he could have benefited from drinking the recommended amount. Similarly, when we first come to spirituality, many of us are attracted by the mystical verses and promises of eternal bliss found in the scriptures and spiritual books; the problem comes when we try to actually put the spiritual principles into practice. We need a Master's advice to know which spiritual practices will be good for us and how much we should practice each day.

The 12th chapter of the *Bhagavad Gita* describes the path of devotion as a progression from *saguna* (with form) to *nirguna* (formless). This rudimentary understanding of the path is essential, of course, but we are able to put it into practice only under the guidance of a living Satguru. The True Master is the culmination of all the teachings we encounter in the scriptures. He not only embodies the teaching, but he also gives the personal contact we need to continue on the path. Though there may be one Buddha or Ramana Maharshi[6] among millions of people, for everyone else it is only possible to transcend the mind and reach the infinite when one has the guidance of a Realized Soul who has already reached that state.

It doesn't take much effort for us to remember how we were before meeting Amma. We may have read some spiritual books and even tried our hand at meditation, but all of our efforts would have been very mediocre compared to what we are able to do in Amma's presence. If we had not met Amma, even now we would probably be in almost the same condition. Until we meet the Guru, all the teachings that we encounter remain as objective concepts, which we are unable to fully imbibe and put into practice. Even if we practice for some time, when difficult

---

[6] Sri Ramana Maharshi, the Sage of Arunachala, realized the Self at the age of 18, after lying down on the floor and imagining what it would be like to die. There are other cases of those who have attained Liberation without the guidance of a Guru, but they are extremely rare. These individuals surely had a Guru in their previous birth, and must have been standing on the brink of Self-realization when they died, needing only a gentle nudge—or needing only to exhaust a small amount of remaining prarabdha—to attain the goal.

circumstances arise in our life, everything will fall apart, and we are back to square one again.

Even those who worship the formless have a Guru to guide them. Nisargdatta Maharaj had a Guru who instructed him in that path, and through simply having strong faith in his Guru's teachings, he was able to reach the goal in a short span of time. Even after becoming established fully in the nondual state, he worshipped the picture of his Guru until his very last breath. Amma says, "A true disciple may say, 'I am one with God,' but he or she will never say, 'I am one with the Guru,' even after realizing his oneness with the entire universe. The disciple knows that it was only the grace of the Guru that enabled him to reach the state of Realization, and because of this, he will always have a feeling of utmost reverence and devotion toward the Guru."

Of course, for most of us, whether we worship God with form or contemplate the formless Brahman, the spiritual path is a long process that requires a lot of patience and hard work. We won't be able to keep up the required level of effort without the constant inspiration and guidance we get through the form of the Guru. Amma offers us this inspiration and guidance, and She always gives it at just the right time. We may be totally despondent and on the verge of giving up all hope, but just one hug or a glance from Amma changes our whole mood and can keep us going for months.

One reason why many people today show a preference for meditation on the formless Absolute is because it seems like a shortcut. Since the Truth is said to be beyond name and form, it may seem faster and more sensible to immediately begin with formless meditation, bypassing the whole process of worshipping a form to gain purity of mind. However, without the proper guidance in this kind of spiritual practice, it is very easy for us to fall prey to our own mind, acting only according to our personal likes and dislikes. Today, most of us don't like being controlled or told what to do. We may feel we already have too many bosses in their lives. Our parents and teachers are our bosses until we grow up, our spouse is our boss after marriage, we have a boss at work, and so forth. Like this, God or the Guru is perceived as just one more boss—the spiritual boss. We may say, "I want peace of mind; I don't want to tremble before some awesome authority figure in the church or temple. Contemplation on the formless is best for me."

This type of attitude, however, comes from a misunderstanding of what God or the Guru is. When one has a living Guru, one's perspective changes completely. We know from our experience that we don't perceive Amma simply as an awesome authority figure. The role of disciplinarian is part of Her existence, but She also plays all the other major roles in our lives: mother, father, beloved, sister, brother, even son and daughter. The disciple knows that whatever the Guru says is for his or her best, and the more the disciple obeys the Guru, the more the Guru pours out his or her grace in the form of further instruction and guidance.

There are myriad disadvantages to practicing meditation on that which has no attributes. First of all, we cannot think of qualities or attributes unrelated to forms. We are only able to understand fully the virtues explained in the scriptures when we observe them through the physical medium that Amma provides. Just try to imagine the sweetness of Amma's smile without Her lips and teeth, or Her compassionate glance without the eyes. The same thing happens when we try to contemplate a formless, changeless, attribute-less God. Since our minds are not subtle enough to do proper contemplation, we need an object that has the quality we are trying to develop as its attribute.

Amma says, "If one dish is served at a restaurant or only one size of shoe is sold at a department store, how many people will find it useful? To suit the tastes and needs of a variety of people, we have to offer various dishes or shoes in a wide variety of sizes. Similarly the Rishis knew that human beings have many differing dispositions. With this in mind, the various deities, differing in qualities and appearance, have been offered as objects of worship. It is good to choose one deity on which to focus our attention, but we should do so with the understanding that just as the same electricity gives power to the refrigerator, the air conditioner, the heater and the light bulb, each deity is a different manifestation of the same divine principle."

There is a story of a brahmachari who came to Amma's ashram as one who meditated on the formless Absolute. One day Amma suddenly took a picture of the goddess Kali from the wall and gave it to him, telling him to meditate on it instead of his present practice. She knew that he used to meditate on Kali and that he had begun his formless meditation simply on the advice of a scholar. Amma said, "You are not mature enough to meditate upon the formless. Therefore, meditate on this form of the Mother. Without love, nothing can be gained. Your mind has become very hard. Sprinkle the water of love and make it soft." The image that Amma gave him was actually of Kali in the same exact pose that he used to meditate on. It was only because he had a Guru like Amma that he was able to avoid the great obstacle that would have occurred in his path.

Amma says, "Temples originated in later periods when the minds of people became too gross to do internal purification alone. The Rishis knew that the people belonging to the forthcoming ages would be unable to grasp these subtle truths unless they were put in a different way." Worship of the form starts as an adoration of a certain personage, then later matures as the worshipper understands the principles and ideals working behind the superficial attributes of their deity. It is a progression from the personal to the impersonal. At the beginning, attachment to form is very important because that is the only way that we can imbibe the essence behind it and assimilate that essence in our lives. Without attachment to Amma's form, we won't be able to gain full exposure to the broad range of Her *bhavas* (moods) and *lilas* (divine plays), which are the medium through which She demonstrates the virtues we need to develop.

About the advanced state of meditation on a form, Amma says: "At a certain stage of spiritual practice, all forms will merge and disappear, and one will reach the Formless State. Supreme devotion is pure Vedanta. A true devotee sees everything as pervaded by God. He does not see anything except God everywhere. When a devotee says, 'Everything is pervaded by God,' the Vedantin says, 'Everything is pervaded by Brahman.'"

Amma compares jumping for the formless without first developing the proper qualities of mind to trying to climb a tree all in one leap. Not only will we fail, but we may fall down and injure ourselves, too. It can also be described by the familiar expression "putting the cart before the horse"—we are not going to go anywhere. To move forward on the spiritual path, we need to put the horse before the cart—that is, to understand the importance of worship with form and accept it as an essential stage in our spiritual practice. A scholar may understand the concept behind the progression from form to formless, but everyone needs a Guru to convert this objective understanding into a real practice in their lives. When the disciple reaches the advanced stages of spiritual practice, it is through the medium of the Guru's form that he or she receives instruction in formless meditation.

We should not take our relationship with Amma for granted. In it lies everything we need; all of spirituality is contained therein. The relationship with the Guru leads us along the spiritual path from beginning to end, gives us all the inspiration we need and removes the obstacles that we encounter along the way. Constant association with the Guru is also the most effective way of removing the ego whenever it surfaces. The Guru will even lead the disciple to formless meditation when he or she is ready. Thus, the Guru leads the disciple beyond the limitations of mind to reach the Supreme State.

Chapter 12

Seeing the Good is Seeing God

Once someone asked Amma, "What is the best way to see God in everyone?" Amma replied that the best way to see God everywhere is to see goodness everywhere. In doing so, we are not fooling ourselves. Amma points out that even a murderer will have feelings of love and concern for his own child. Thus there is goodness in everyone. Amma says that this goodness is God.

While Amma sees only the good in everyone, at present most of us are able to see only the faults in others. Many years ago, a devotee came to Amma because he was having serious financial problems with his company. Even though he knew that the ashram was financially strapped at that time, he was hoping that Amma would somehow help him. He promised that he would return the money when his company started making a profit again. Seeing his miserable condition, Amma helped him even though it meant more hardship for the ashram.

A few of us did not like that Amma was giving money when we had so little. I was the chief cashier in a bank at that time and was very concerned about the ashram's financial situation. When the man did not return the money even after his business had stabilized, some of the brahmacharis living in the ashram became agitated and wanted to force him to give back the money. Without saying anything to Amma, a few of us went to his house and pressured him to return the money. Using strong words, we insisted that he return the money immediately or face the consequences. Our efforts were to no avail.

Before we took a more extreme step, I went to Amma to ask Her what we should do. Amma calmly replied, "So what if he doesn't return the money? He's also my son, just like you, isn't he?"

By pursuing this matter, I thought that I had been showing my sincerity and interest in helping the ashram. After hearing Amma's response, I felt like a punctured balloon. Whereas I had been seeing only the money and was judging the man for not returning it, Amma was seeing us all equally. Amma always says that it is the negative actions of the person that are to be condemned and not the person himself. This is because, in essence, everyone is the same Atman.

When we are used to focusing only on what we don't like in a person or situation, we can even reach a point when we can no longer appreciate what is truly valuable to us.

Once a married man was working in his office, looking over some building plans with his secretary. Sitting close to her, he didn't notice that one of her long dark hairs stuck to his white dress shirt. When he returned home, his wife saw the secretary's hair on his shirt and began crying.

"Oh, now I can see the proof that you've been having an affair with your secretary!"

Noticing the hair for the first time, the man tried to explain, but to no avail. The next day, before returning home, he made sure that no hair was sticking to any of his clothes. Just before reaching home, he saw someone walking a big dog with long, golden fur. The dog took a liking to him, and he couldn't resist petting it. The dog rubbed up against the man's leg and tried to lick him. At that time, a few long, golden strands of hair stuck to his pants, but he didn't notice.

He entered the house with a bouquet of roses in his hand, saying, "Honey, I'm home!"

His wife did not look up; she was scrutinizing every inch of his clothing for stray hairs. When she saw the dog's golden hairs, she immediately burst into tears.

"What, honey? What's wrong?"

"I see the blonde hair on your pants! I can see that now you're not only having an affair with your secretary, but with my best friend, too!"

The man was at his wits' end. The next day he made sure that not a single speck of dust was on his clothes anywhere. He also made sure to cross the street whenever he saw a person walking a dog. Knowing that he had taken every necessary precaution, he entered his house confidently calling, "Hi, honey! I'm home!" with a box of gourmet chocolates in one hand and tickets for a vacation to Hawaii in the other.

But his wife again scrutinized him from head to toe. After scanning every inch of his body and finding nothing, she broke into a wail even louder than before.

"What's wrong, honey? There's no hair sticking to me, right?"

"Yes, I can see that," the wife said between sobs, "Having an affair with your secretary was bad, with my best friend worse, but I never thought you would start seeing a bald woman!"

In this way, sometimes even when others try to show us love, if our hearts are closed we won't be able to accept it. The following story from the Jewish tradition shows the value of seeing the good in every situation that life brings us.

Rabbi Moshe took a trip to a strange land. He took a donkey, a rooster and a lamp. One night he was refused hospitality by every house in a particular village. Having no other choice, he decided to sleep in the woods.

He lit his lamp to study the holy books before going to sleep, but a fierce wind came up, knocking over the lamp and breaking it. The rabbi decided to turn in, saying, "All that God does, he does well." During the night some wild animals came along and drove away the rooster, and thieves stole the donkey. Even when the rabbi woke up and saw the losses he had sustained, he still proclaimed easily, "All that God does, he does well."

The rabbi then went back to the village where he had been refused lodging, only to learn that enemy soldiers had invaded it during the night and killed all the inhabitants. He also learned that these soldiers had traveled through the same part of the woods where he lay asleep. Had his lamp not been broken, he would have been discovered. Had the rooster not been chased off, it would have crowed, giving him away. Likewise, had not the donkey been stolen, its braying would have betrayed him. Once more Rabbi Moshe declared, "All that God does, he does well!"

This strategy works both ways. When we are able to see God everywhere, we will see the good in everyone and remember that each person and object is a valuable part of God's creation.

One day the Sage Adi Shankaracharya came upon a low-caste person, traditionally seen as untouchable. Shankaracharya asked him to move aside so he could continue on his path. Without moving, the untouchable asked the Sage, "What is it you want to move from the path? This body or the indwelling Self?" He continued, "Oh, Great Ascetic, you have established that the Absolute is everywhere, in you and in me. Is it this body, made up of the five elements, that you wish to keep at a distance from that body, which is also made up of the five elements? Or do you wish to separate the pure Awareness which is present here from the same Awareness that is present there?"

Shankaracharya immediately recognized his mistake. Bowing low to him, he composed five verses on the spot, stating that whoever exhibited such equal vision, though he might be an untouchable, was indeed his Guru. When the Sage had completed the verses, the untouchable disappeared and there in his place stood Lord Shiva, the primordial Guru.

Many people argue, if there is a God, why is there so much suffering in the world? Amma says that in God's creation, there is no suffering. At the level of human beings, there is both sorrow and happiness, pleasure and pain. But at God's level, there is neither sorrow nor happiness, only bliss. That is why the scriptures refer to the Supreme Being as *anandaswarupam*, or "of the form of bliss." It is only human beings who have created suffering. The following story illustrates this point.

Once, someone complained to the sun, "Why do you always leave half the world in darkness? If you really loved the world, wouldn't there be light everywhere?"

When the sun heard this, he was really confused and concerned. He asked the person, "Really, is there a part of the world that is in darkness? Can you show it to me?"

The person agreed and led the sun around the world to see the darkness on the other side. But wherever the sun went, there was only light. Finally the sun had gone all the way around the world and had not seen darkness anywhere.

Asking God why there is so much suffering in the world is like asking the sun why there is darkness. Where the sun is, there is no darkness. Likewise, from the point of view of one who has realized his or her True Self, there is no suffering.

We all have so many problems and complaints. In the days and weeks before we know we are going to see Amma, we may start to tabulate a mental list of grievances to share with Her when we receive Her darshan. But what happens? More often than not, the moment we reach Amma's lap, we cannot think of any problems at all. All our suffering seems to evaporate. The Master is like a mirror that reflects our True Self. In Amma's presence, we get a taste of that which is beyond sorrow, and beyond happiness, too—that is the bliss of the Self.

Instead of looking at our problems from a negative angle, if we approach every situation with a positive frame of mind, much can be gained. Jacques Lusseyran, a French university professor who was blinded at the age of eight and 10 years later suffered the worst horrors of human evil in a Nazi concentration camp, later wrote, "Joy does not come from outside, for whatever happens to us it is within." If Lusseyran could find inner peace even under those most horrific of circumstances, we definitely have the capacity to transcend every form of difficulty in our own lives and experience bliss within no matter what our external circumstances may be.

Several years ago, a traveler came to Amma's ashram in India somewhat by coincidence and stayed for some time. I didn't see him at any of the regular programs during the first few days, so feeling a bit concerned, I asked him how he was enjoying his stay.

He said, "It is a very peaceful place, but there are a few things that get on my nerves."

"Really?" I asked him. "What are those?"

"Well," the visitor explained, "I get up real early in the morning to meditate, but this terrible racket starts in the temple." He was talking about the archana. "Then everything is nice and quiet until about 11:00 a.m. or so. Then again so many people are bustling around inside the temple, singing and making noise." By this, he was referring to Amma's darshan. "Then, again, it is nice and peaceful for some time until they start singing those noisy songs in the evening." This comment was referring to Amma's bhajans. "Overall, though, I feel very peaceful here, so I can't bring myself to leave."

The traveler didn't realize that everything he disliked about the ashram—archana, Amma's darshan and the bhajans—were the very things that create the peaceful, holy atmosphere he enjoyed so much.

After talking to this traveler, I was reminded of the story that one of Amma's brahmacharis told me about his experience visiting a monastery in Japan. Upon entering the complex, the brahmachari was immediately struck by the idyllic location and the very peaceful surroundings. Later, the brahmachari told me that as he entered the monastery's grounds, he felt a momentary twinge of envy. He thought to himself, "How fortunate these people are to have such a peaceful, meditative atmosphere in which to do their spiritual practices. Look at me, I don't get to stay in one place much, and even when I do, it is in Tokyo. When we are in Amritapuri it is so crowded, and when we are with Amma, everything is so hectic. This is such a nice place…"

However, as the brahmachari got to speaking with the monastery's head monk, many interesting facts about their situation were revealed. The head monk said that they were facing a variety of problems on numerous levels. There were, of course, the interpersonal struggles and conflicts that arise whenever ego-bound souls congregate in numbers of two or higher anywhere. Then they were also facing legal problems and financial troubles.

The head monk continued to clarify, "Actually all these problems are really insignificant, compared to our most serious problem."

The brahmachari asked him, "What is that?"

The head monk replied, "It is a problem that weighs heavily on the minds of many monks in Japan today. The whole tradition here is facing a serious crisis, in that there are almost no living Realized Masters remaining."

Listening to the head monk, the brahmachari realized that no matter how serene the setting seemed to be, there was no peace in the minds of those staying there. Whereas, while Amma's ashram (which Amma has even compared to a jungle) often appears chaotic, the ashramites are being trained to be at peace within, no matter what the external circumstances might be. The primary difference between the monastery in Japan and Amma's ashram, however, was not the decibel level but the presence of a Realized Master. Without a Master, it is difficult to lead an authentic spiritual life even in the most peaceful of surroundings.

As we progress along the spiritual path, we tend to vacillate between overconfidence and despair. We either think that we are already perfect or that there's no hope. Ideally, we should recognize our present incomplete state, but have full faith that Amma will lead us to the goal—we need both patience and enthusiasm.

While Beethoven was still a young man, all but unknown to the world, he began to lose his hearing, and he was struggling with his musical studies. Around the same time, his father passed away. He became very depressed and even contemplated suicide. Now, let us imagine that you could go back in time and meet our depressed Beethoven at this critical juncture. He is totally miserable and lacks confidence, but you know his hidden talent. What would you say to him? "Yeah, Ludwig, you're right. It's hopeless. You're just wasting your time with all this practice and everything. Give up." Of course nobody would say such a thing because they would know what an immeasurable loss that would be to the world. Without a doubt, we would do everything within our capacity to encourage him to practice relentlessly.

Just like Beethoven, we are unaware of the latent power and greatness within us. Each of us carries within us the symphony of eternal joy and peace. We tend to think only of our limitations, but Amma always sees only the infinite potential beyond that and strives to unearth it.

Many brahmacharis working in Amma's Amrita Kuteeram (free houses for the homeless poor) project had no prior experience in construction. Some of them were truly surprised when Amma asked them to begin building and supervising the construction of houses. But with Amma's grace they were able to learn very quickly, and now they are competently managing even large-scale development projects like slum rehabilitation and the rebuilding of entire communities devastated by natural disasters.

When it became clear that Amma's super-specialty hospital in Cochin needed a digital hospital information system, the hospital administrators came to Amma with the prices for existing systems designed by multinational corporations. Such systems do not come cheaply. When Amma saw the bids, She said, "We will develop our own hospital information system," and named one of the brahmacharis as the developer in-charge. The hospital administrators could not believe their ears. The brahmachari Amma had selected to develop the system had the right formal qualifications but not much hands-on experience, and such systems typically take years and whole teams of software-technology experts to develop. The administrators were convinced Amma was making a big mistake, but they had no choice but to go along with Her decision. Within a year, the system was up and running, and the administrators had to admit that it was equal to or better than the systems they had been looking into buying for a huge sum.

It is very easy for a carpenter to use shiny new nails, but imagine the task of a carpenter who has only rusty, bent nails to work with. Out of Her infinite compassion, Amma chooses all of us rusty, bent nails and with tremendous patience, works to polish and straighten us.

There is a verse of Adi Shankaracharya in the *Shiva Aparadha Kshamapana Stotram* that explains our real state: "I am not able to perform the duty consisting of rituals prescribed in the scriptures since it is beset at every step with complex rites. Much less is my ability to perform the prescribed duty by the Vedic injunctions leading to the essential path of the realization of Brahman. There is no desire in me for knowing and performing dharma. Nor have I any idea about listening to the import of the Vedas from the Guru and reflecting on it. What(object)remains there for me to meditate upon leading to Self-realization? Oh, my Lord, please forgive me for all these faults and accept me out of Your infinite mercy."

Once Amma was giving advice to some Westerners who were suffering as they struggled to live a spiritual life amidst all the problems and challenges of their day-to-day lives. She said, "During this process, one might fail many times. Let failures happen. After all, failure comes only to a person who tries for success. But do not lose your enthusiasm and interest. Try again and again. Declare an open war with your mind. The mind might pull you and push you into the same old habits. Understand that it is only a trick of the greatest trickster, the mind, to divert you from the path. Do not give up. There will come a point when the vasanas will lose all their strength and give way for the Lord to come in and rule. Till then try and keep trying. Let all the failures fail to stop you from continuing your practice."

It is because Amma understands our inner potential far more than we do that She never gives up Her efforts to guide and mold Her children. We may give up on ourselves, but She will never give up on us. Knowing that Amma will never give up on us, let us pray that we can have enough faith in the divine presence within us to persevere with patience and enthusiasm until we reach the goal.

Amma knows that we are all good and pure in essence. No matter how many faults we may have, She knows that we, too, are on the path to Realization. When Amma says that She sees God everywhere, She could just as easily say She sees good everywhere. As Amma continually nurtures the goodness within us, this goodness strengthens and grows brighter. Just as a sculptor creates a beautiful statue out of a shapeless hunk of stone, Amma slowly strips away our negative qualities and tendencies, allowing our innate divinity and beauty to shine forth.

Chapter 13

Where and How to Start Sharing Love

When we think about all that Amma has given us, naturally we will want to do our best to give something back. Then the question arises: how can we ever repay Amma for all that She has given us? The truth is that it is an impossible task—we can never repay Her. Amma is giving us infinite, unconditional love and compassion. To repay an infinite gift, we should respond in kind. As long as our awareness remains confined to the finite, limited ego, we will never be able to give an infinite gift. Whenever anyone asks Amma what She would like, She replies that She doesn't need anything, but if we truly love Her, we will express love and compassion toward all beings.

We may feel that we are overburdened with too many responsibilities and problems and we have neither the time nor the energy to do good for others. The following story shows that we can always find ways to help others, no matter what our circumstances may be.

Once an old widower wanted to till his garden, but he was no longer strong enough for so much physical exertion.

His only child, who otherwise would have helped him, was serving time in prison as a convicted jewel thief. The old man wrote the following letter to his son:

Dear Son,
I am feeling pretty bad because it looks like I won't be
able to plant my garden this year. I hate to miss doing the
garden, because your mother always loved planting time.
I'm just getting too old to be digging up a garden plot. If
you were here, all my troubles would be over. I know you
would dig the plot for me, if you weren't in prison.
Love,
Your Dad

A few days later, the old man received the following note from his son:

For God's sake, Dad, don't dig up the garden! That's
where I buried the jewels!

At 4:00 a.m. the next morning, a dozen police officers showed up and dug up the entire garden but did not find any jewels. Confused, the old man wrote another note to his son, telling him what had happened and asking him what to do next.

His son's reply was:

Go ahead and plant your potatoes, Dad... It was the best
I could do from here.

Amma says that we should try to make at least one person happy every day, either through giving some kind of physical or financial assistance to them, listening to their sorrows or sharing our talents with them. If we feel that are not able to offer anything to others, we can at least present a smiling face to all those who cross our path. Amma tells the following story about the value of a smile.

There was a very depressed person on his way home from the office. He had had a bad day at work. As he was waiting at the bus stop, he was feeling really down in the dumps. Also waiting at the bus stop was a kind and gentle lady who smiled sympathetically at our depressed office worker.

He had never experienced that kind of a smile in his life. Like the sun breaking through dark clouds, this smile was a ray of light piercing the depression and despair hanging over his mind. Standing in the light of the stranger's compassionate smile, he suddenly felt very happy, and this happiness stayed with him as he boarded the bus and began his journey home.

After getting down from the bus, he saw a beggar huddled on the street. As he was still feeling so happy from receiving the stranger's smile, he gave the beggar everything he had in his pockets. The beggar took the money and after filling his stomach and having a hot cup of coffee, decided to buy a lottery ticket. When the beggar scratched off the ticket, he saw that he had won a modest prize. It wasn't much, but it was more than the beggar usually had, and he knew that he would not have to worry about what to eat for the next few days. This filled him with a sense of relief and happiness as he began to walk back to his village.

On his way he saw a small, sick, emaciated dog that looked near the point of death. Seeing the dog's plight, the beggar felt very sad. Normally he would not have been affected, but because he had been feeling so happy and blessed with good fortune, he was overcome with compassion when he saw this dog suffering. He picked up the dog and cradled it in his arms as he walked toward his home. On the way, he bought some food for the dog. It was the first time the dog had eaten in many days. After eating, it became a little stronger and more alert. When night fell, the beggar still had not reached his village, so he stopped in the house of a family which sometimes took him in. The beggar and the dog retired to the garage of the house to sleep.

During the night, the house suddenly caught fire. Everyone was fast asleep and would have died but for the dog that woke up and started barking. The dog's barking alerted all the members of the household, and everyone escaped unscathed. This family had two children, one of whom later became a Mahatma and showered his blessings on thousands of spiritual seekers and those seeking solace. If the kindhearted lady at the bus stop had not smiled at the depressed office worker, this Mahatma would have perished in his sleep and the world would have gone without his divine blessings. This is the power of a single smile. As Amma once said, "Even things that are bound to happen after 20,000 years—even a small event—even now its seed is present." When we think about how profoundly even the smallest of our actions can affect the world, how can we continue to hold back the love and kindness within us?

Even if we give a small gift, if we give it with love, it can have a very positive effect in a person's life. Sometimes small children bring their drawings to Amma. If you look at the paper, there is nothing more than two or three lines, just some chicken scratches, but they offer it to Amma with so much love. Amma often accepts these drawings by touching them to Her head. In India, this is a way of showing one's appreciation and respect for something holy and feeling that the grace and goodness is coming to one's whole body. Of course, the gift may be insignificant; what is Amma going to do with all these drawings? But Amma considers even these small children's scribblings as holy because they were drawn and given to Her with love.

If given with love, even an insignificant gift can become great, but without love even if we give expensive and elaborate gifts, they are not going to be appreciated and they won't have much of an effect on the other person. For instance, a business gives its clients so many gifts, but these are not given with love, only with the intention that the clients will remain loyal to the company. The clients know very well that they are an asset to the company, and they have come to expect that every year the company will give them gifts. This kind of gift cannot even be called a gift. Rather, it is a form of bartering.

Amma says that if one is able to give real love, that love makes the giver a saintly person. This love is both the cause and the consequence of spiritual growth. When we are able to share love with others, we grow spiritually. The more we grow spiritually, the more we are able to share love.

How can we start to practice giving the gift of love? I would say the best place to start is where you are now. Don't think that if you want to be spiritual you have to become a *sannyasin* (monk). If you have a family, the best place to practice this gift is in your own home. Your children are right there; your spouse is right there. Practice being more loving with them.

Amma says that sharing love doesn't necessarily mean embracing everyone. To give love means to give our time, to give our attention, to show others that we care for them, that we are concerned for their welfare, their happiness and their unhappiness. Practicing like this creates a wonderful atmosphere in the family. If you live alone, try to share your concern, time and attention with your coworkers and friends. Wherever you are, don't expect others to be as loving as you are. Typically, if one person does not receive the expected response from the other, their love immediately diminishes. We should not forget that at present, our relationship is between two ignorant people. Each one is expecting to receive unconditional love and attention from the other, while neither one is able to give selfless love. Instead of dwelling on the fact that your partner cannot give you the kind of love you are looking for and feeling guilty that you yourself are not able to give pure love, try to take comfort in the fact that you are doing the best you can.

Frequently I visit the homes of Amma's devotees. There are often complaints from the husband, complaints from the wife and complaints from the children. The wife blames her husband, the husband blames his wife, the children blame their parents. All this is because the family is not giving enough time and attention to each other. Sometimes the wife is talking and the husband is watching TV. He tells her, "Go on, I am listening to you," but even while he tells her that, he doesn't take his eyes off the TV. How is the wife going to feel satisfied that she is being listened to?

The judge in the Mullah Nasrudin's village had gone on vacation. As per the local rules, the Mullah was asked to be the judge for a day. The Mullah sat behind the judge's podium, gavel in hand, gazing sternly down at the audience. Finally he ordered the first case brought for hearing.

"You are right," said the Mullah, after hearing one side of the argument.

"You are right," he said, after hearing the other side.

"But both sides cannot be right," protested a voice from the audience.

"You are right," said the Mullah.

Similarly, we all think we are right and that the other person is the source of the problem. The husband thinks his wife is wrong, and the wife thinks her husband is wrong. The real problem is the absence of sincere love, concern and attention for each other. If there is an atmosphere of love in our family, even if we have a problem in our life, when we come home we'll feel so relieved. But now the situation is the reverse. We have so many problems in our life outside, and when we come home we have even more problems. That's why many people don't come home after work; they hang out somewhere and come home only late at night when everyone is fast asleep.

Try to think that God has given you a family. Remember that there are so many people who want to have a family, but they are not able to get married. Even if they get married, after two years the wife may leave the husband, or the husband may leave the wife. Even if they remain together, they may not be able to have children. To have a family, you need God's grace. So if you have a family, that is the best place to begin sharing the gift of love. Amma always says that She wants all of us to do our best to share this love, to give our time and attention especially to our family members. Once we have been able to do this within our family, we can slowly extend our love to our friends, to society as a whole, and finally to all of creation. Ultimately, we can become an embodiment of Amma's love so that whoever comes near us will also be able to feel Her love.

Chapter 14

Sacred Work

Many people tell me that after being with Amma for a few days, they find it very painful to be away from Her physical presence. Compared to being with Amma, all worldly activities seem dull and empty. But the fact is that most of us have many responsibilities that we cannot run away from. We may have children, a spouse or elderly parents who are depending on us. If we lose all our strength and enthusiasm thinking that everything we do is just a waste of time, our loved ones may suffer.

In ancient times there was an Indian king named Shivaji. King Shivaji had built his own kingdom by winning territory back from the Mughals who had invaded India and established their own empire. However, in order to preserve his kingdom he had to continually fight off the Mughal invaders. Over the years he grew weary of war and bloodshed, no matter how noble his cause. One day, when Shivaji's Guru came before him and asked for *bhiksha* (alms), Shivaji wrote something on a slip of paper and handed it to his Guru.

His Guru rebuked him, saying, "I am a sannyasin, I need only food. I cannot eat paper."

Shivaji said, "On this paper I have signed over my entire kingdom and all its wealth to you. You have come for alms, and that is what I have given. I want no more of this world and its precious wealth, fame and power."

The Guru said, "You have offered this kingdom to me, and I accept it. Now the kingdom belongs to me."

With a sigh of tremendous relief, Shivaji prostrated at his Guru's feet, feeling that literally the weight of the world had been lifted from his shoulders. He then asked his Guru what he should do with the rest of his life.

"I want you to take care of the kingdom, to be its steward. You will rule this kingdom as my representative," the Guru instructed Shivaji.

Thus Shivaji remained as the ruler of the kingdom, but he did so in his Guru's name. Though he carried out all the same tasks he had previously done, his attitude was completely different. Rather than feeling, "I am the lord of the land," he told himself, "This is not my kingdom anymore; I am just a caretaker who is serving his Guru." In this way all the tension he had been experiencing was removed, and there was much more love and attention in his actions as well. Even today, Shivaji is renowned as one of the greatest kings in human history.

Likewise, we need not give up the work we are doing now. All that is needed to transform our life is a change in our attitude. If we can think that Amma has given us our work and do it as a service to Her, we will be able to discharge our responsibilities with love and sincerity. That in itself is a life dedicated to Amma.

Before Amma asked Ron Gottsegen to become the administrative director of AIMS, Her super-specialty hospital in Cochin, he used to read only scriptures and scriptural commentaries. But when he took up this responsibility, he had to read many technical books related to medicine, medical technology and hospital administration. After two or three years of this, he began to feel sorry that he had no time at all to study scriptures anymore. Instead of learning about the Atman, he was learning about the MRI. One day he told Amma that after all these years of studying the *Upanishads*, the *Bhagavad Gita* and other spiritual treasures, he was afraid he was wasting his time in reading all these technical books.

Amma's beautiful reply can benefit us all. Amma told him, "This is the work I have given you for the time being. Don't worry whether it is going to help you in your spiritual pursuit or not. If you are doing your work sincerely, that is serving the Guru—it will certainly benefit you spiritually."

Whatever a Mahatma like Amma does is only to restore the lost harmony in society and creation as a whole. Whenever Amma founds a new institution—be it a hospital, business school, orphanage, or medical college—it is always done to create more order and harmony in society. For instance, before Amma took over the orphanage in Paripally, Kerala that is now run by Her ashram, the children there were wallowing in despair, scraping by in unlivable conditions. When Amma adopted this orphanage, She remodeled it and completely rebuilt its infrastructure and care program, thus bringing harmony to a place that had been the epitome of disharmony and sorrow. When She constructed Her super-specialty hospital in Cochin, it was in response to the cold hard fact that in Kerala (and many other parts of India), if one needed a specialized operation to survive and did not have the money to pay for it, there was no hope for survival. Now, not only do poor patients have AIMS as a recourse in times of need, but many hospitals in Kerala have been forced to lower their prices to stay competitive. Here again, Amma created dharma out of adharma, harmony out of disharmony. In all of Am-ma's institutions combined, there are thousands of employees, and many thousands more who serve voluntarily. By virtue of working in one of these institutions or projects, one's actions are contributing toward restoring harmony in society and the world. Not only are these institutions a great service to society, but each individual volunteer and employee benefits spiritually. The scriptures say, "Whoever is contributing to the universal harmony is worshipping God; whoever disturbs the harmony goes against God."

Of course, this does not only apply to those working in Amma's institutions. Any one of us can adopt this attitude toward our work, no matter what we do. Amma advised me in the same way when I was working in a bank. Though my work had no relationship with the ashram whatsoever, because I was able to think that Amma put me in that position, that Amma had given me that job, and that each customer who came to me was personally sent by Amma, I was able to treat the customers with so much more patience, understanding and affection. That, itself, is serving the Guru. Amma says that to truly love Her is to love and serve all beings. So wherever we are, whatever work we are doing, if we are able to treat our coworkers and others with kindness and love, imagining that Amma has placed us in that particular situation to do exactly that, we are indeed leading a spiritual life.

It is only a question of changing our attitude. As long as we are able to perform our work with love and sincerity, that becomes our service to the Guru. Without that, spirituality becomes the domain of sannyasins alone. But spirituality is not for a limited few—it is for everyone. Actually, it is the most practical of all sciences. The scriptures and the Spiritual Masters know that most people are busy fulfilling their responsibilities to others, and they will not be able to retire into an ashram or a lonely place to fill their time with spiritual practices. How then can they incorporate spirituality into their day-to-day life?

For the answer, we need look no further than Amma. Though She has no biological children, it can be said that Amma has the world's biggest family—millions of devotees consider Amma their Mother, and in fact She sees all beings in creation as Her children. Therefore we can say that Amma has more worldly responsibilities than anyone else on the planet. But Amma never thinks, "Let me finish my work for the day and then do some spiritual practice." Though Amma is ever engaged in action, She never sees anything as different from Her spiritual practice. In each person that comes to Her, She sees God. In each person's ear, She chants the name of the Divine Mother. Amma is the living proof that though we have so many responsibilities and obligations, it is possible to lead a spiritual life in the world.

Amma says that though She loves everyone equally, She feels a special affection for those who work for others, rather than those who work for themselves. As part of Her keynote address to the 2004 Parliament of World's Religions in Barcelona, Amma said that if we have at least a little compassion in our hearts, we will work an extra half an hour each day to earn money for the poor and needy. Amma said that in this way a solution to all the sorrow and poverty in the world will be revealed. Even if we feel that our job is totally unrelated to Amma's organization and the work She is carrying out, if we make the commitment to work half an hour each day purely for the sake of those in need, whatever job we have becomes karma yoga. Just by following this one simple instruction from Amma, our entire working life becomes an offering to God—the mundane becomes sacred.

Once the denizens of Hell lodged a complaint with God. "We have been suffering in Hell for so many centuries," they explained to God. "And whenever we look up, we can see the residents of Heaven enjoying all the celestial pleasures and having such a wonderful time."

God listened patiently. "I'll see what I can do," He said. Then He went to the residents of Heaven and told them about the complaint of the denizens of Hell. Without even being asked, the residents of Heaven generously offered to trade places with them.

Of course, the denizens of Hell took them up on their offer. And so it was that everyone who had heretofore been enjoying the pleasures of Heaven descended into Hell, and all those who had been suffering in Hell ascended to the celestial realm.

Two weeks later, God went to Heaven to see how the new residents were faring. But when He got there, He didn't recognize the place. The new residents were not taking care of it at all. They had stopped cleaning the streets and the houses, and it looked like they had not had a bath since arriving in Heaven. It could have been said that the crime rate was on the rise, but actually it was the first time there had ever been a crime rate in Heaven. The people did not smile at each other as they passed one another in the street. Feelings of fear, doubt, hatred and despair reigned supreme. In fact, after just two weeks, Heaven was starting to look a lot like Hell.

Then God descended to Hell to ask the former residents of Heaven what they thought should be done about the state of affairs in Heaven. After all, since they had willingly given up the place, there was nothing to stop them from taking it back, either.

Just as He had not recognized Heaven after two weeks of occupation by the former denizens of Hell, the same could be said of their old stomping grounds. The former residents of Heaven had been hard at work—cleaning, remodeling and repainting everything in sight. They were all helping each other and no one had the feeling that they would not clean up a mess they hadn't made. As such, the entire place was permeated with feelings of community spirit, mutual support, optimism and good cheer. In fact, God mused, Hell was starting to look a lot like Heaven.

The denizens of Hell thought all their problems would be solved if they could just switch places with their celestial peers. But in the end, it became clear that the qualities of Heaven and Hell were not determined by the real estate, but by the attitudes and actions of their residents. In just two weeks, the residents of Heaven transformed Hell into a place very much like Heaven, while the denizens of Hell had transformed Heaven into another kind of Hell.

Regardless of whether we live at Amma's ashram or are at work in the world, our attitude is the primary determining factor of our experience. Peace, love, patience, compassion—if we cultivate them within us, we will be in heaven even if we are put in an external hell. Whereas if we allow negative qualities like jealousy, anger, impatience and hatred to fester within us, we will find ourselves in hell no matter how pleasant, comfortable, or spiritual our external circumstances may appear to be.

Part 3

Shower of Grace

Grace is always falling like rain.
We just have to become open to receive it.

– Amma

Chapter 15

Amma's Omniscience

We learned early on that it was impossible to hide anything from Amma. At first, this was a surprise to us. We didn't have any previous knowledge about Mahatmas or the characteristics of a Realized Master, so in the beginning we did not understand that Amma was omniscient. And although She never directly informed us that She was, She gave us many experiences demonstrating Her all-knowing nature.

From the earliest days of the ashram, Amma always insisted that all the devotees visiting the ashram be fed before the brahmacharis; the last to take food was always Amma. On many days there was not enough food left after all the devotees had eaten. On some days there was rice but no curry; on other days curry but no rice. Sometimes when there was only rice but nothing to eat it with, we used to put curry powder on the rice to give it some taste. On one such occasion about 25 years ago, two of the brahmacharis were in the kitchen while Amma was giving darshan and found that there was a pot of rice remaining but no curry. Helping themselves to a plate of rice each, they poured curry powder over the top. Perhaps due to their hunger, or else out of carelessness, they poured way too much curry powder over the rice. At that moment, they heard Amma coming toward the kitchen. They knew that Amma would be upset if She saw how much curry powder they had wasted.[1] In order to conceal their mistake, they hastily scooped more rice over the top of the rice that was already covered in curry powder and hid the two plates in a corner of the room behind a door.

When Amma entered the room, one of the brahmacharis had crossed his arms and was humming a tune as casually as possible as if nothing had happened. The other was not so successful at concealing his guilt. He was careful not to meet Amma's eyes and pretended to be searching for something in the opposite corner of the room to where the plates had been stashed.

However, Amma was not fooled for an instant. She made a beeline for the corner where the plates were kept, brushed aside the "decoy" rice and exposed the huge pile of curry powder on top.

Early in his relationship with Amma, Swami Purnamritananda (then a young man named Sreekumar) had an experience that removed any doubt in his mind about Amma's omniscience.

As a young boy, Swami Purnamritananda happened to go to a flute concert. It touched his heart, and he wanted to learn how to play the flute. However, his father did not allow him to do so. He did not want Swami Purnamritananda to divert attention from his studies. Swami Purnamritananda became very sad. One day there was a festival in a nearby temple. He saw a man there playing the flute beautifully with many other flutes for sale. Swami

---

[1] In those days, Amma would sometimes even have to go to neighboring houses asking for rice in order to have something to feed the brahmacharis, so even a handful of curry powder was precious. Even today, when the ashram has over 3,000 residents and serves tens of thousands daily, Amma is careful to instill in the ashram residents a culture of reverence and respect for food and, in fact, all supplies which the ashram makes use of. Because of this the ashram produces an incredibly small amount of waste for an institution of its size.

Purnamritananda bought one and tried to play it himself, but it was extremely difficult. He told his grandmother he wanted someone to teach him how to play the flute. She advised him to pray to the divine flute player, Lord Krishna, to teach him how to play.

The young Swami Purnamritananda believed Her. He went to a Krishna temple and prayed to Krishna to become his flute master. As if the Lord heard his prayer, Swami Purnamritananda was suddenly able to play simple songs.

Many years later, soon after meeting Amma, Swami Purnamritananda decided to test Her. During one Krishna Bhava, he wrapped his flute in newspaper and brought it to the old temple where Amma always gave darshan. He showed it to Amma and asked whether She could identify what was inside.

She smiled and told him, "You tell me, my son."

"I already know what is inside," he replied. "I want to hear it from you."

Amma insisted that he should tell Her. Finally, he had to tell Her that it was his bamboo flute. He was disappointed that Amma was not able to recognize it.

Without missing a beat, Amma gently contradicted him. "It is not a flute, my child, but a packet of incense sticks."

Swami Purnamritananda was sure that he was correct. "No, it is my flute. I packed it myself."

Amma asked him to remove the wrapping. All the devotees watched with great curiosity as he removed the newspaper. Instead of his flute, he was shocked to see a brand-new metallic cylindrical incense case—full of incense sticks.

Swami Purnamritananda couldn't believe his eyes. How could such a thing happen? He mentally asked Amma, "Are you a magician? Why did you turn my flute into a case of incense sticks?" He did not want to test Amma anymore, but he really wanted to get his flute back. He said to Amma humbly, "Please tell me where my flute is."

With a mischievous smile on Her face, Amma said, "It is there in the puja room in your house behind the photo of Krishna." Swami Purnamritananda returned home immediately, went inside the puja room and searched for his flute.

He found it exactly where Amma had described. "How can it be?" he wondered and carefully recollected the day's events. That day, after he had packed the flute and was about to leave the house, his mother had called him to the kitchen. She had insisted that he eat breakfast before leaving.

Swami Purnamritananda had obediently gone to the kitchen after keeping his flute on the living-room table. It had been exactly at that time that his father had come back from the shop, having purchased a cylindrical case full of incense sticks, which was also wrapped in newspaper. He had put it down on the living-room table next to Swami Purnamritananda's flute and gone to the bathroom to wash his feet before entering the puja room.

After coming out of the bathroom, instead of taking the incense packet, he took the similarly wrapped flute and placed it behind the photo of Krishna, which was the usual spot where he would keep incense.

After returning from the kitchen, Swami Purnamritananda picked up the packet of incense sticks, thinking it was the flute that he was going to use to test Amma.

This indeed was what had happened, but there was no way Amma could have known about this sequence of events. Swami Purnamritananda was sure that Amma, aware of his desire to test Her, had orchestrated the events of the day as a mischievous prank on him instead. Prank or no prank, however, he was left with no doubt about Amma's all-knowing nature, and he decided to stop testing Amma.

In the epic *Mahabharata*, there is an incident that took place while the Pandava brothers were living in exile in a forest far from home. One day, Lord Krishna went there to see all of them. Arjuna and Krishna were carrying on a conversation. Pointing to a tree, Krishna asked Arjuna, "Arjuna, do you see that crow sitting there?"

Arjuna said, "Yes, my Lord."

Krishna said, "Arjuna, I think it is not a crow but a cuckoo bird."

Arjuna replied, "Yes, my Lord, it is a cuckoo bird."

Then Krishna seemed to correct himself, saying instead, "Actually, Arjuna, it is not a cuckoo bird, but a baby peacock."

"Oh yes, I can see now that it is a beautiful baby peacock," said Arjuna.

Finally Krishna concluded, "Arjuna, it is neither a crow, nor a cuckoo bird, nor a baby peacock. It is an eagle. Why did you support me when I said all those other things when you could clearly see with your own eyes what type of bird it was?"

Arjuna replied, "My Lord, You are God Himself; thus, You can easily make a crow into a cuckoo bird, a cuckoo bird into a baby peacock, and a baby peacock into an eagle. I know that Your vision is always more correct than mine."

Once, many years back, when I was translating for Amma during one of Her programs in Tamil Nadu, Amma interrupted me and said that I had made a mistake in the translation. I confidently informed Amma that I had studied Tamil in school for 14 years and there was no doubt that I was correct. Suddenly Amma asked me to get up from the stage, saying, "You don't need to do the translation for me," and called one of the devotees who was listening from the audience and asked him to do it. Sadly, I got up from my place but remained within earshot of Amma.

Before the devotee continued the translation, Amma asked him what I had said. He repeated my words, and hearing him I understood that I had made a mistake. Amma had said one thing, and I had said something else. Even though I knew both Malayalam and Tamil well, I hadn't really communicated what Amma had meant. I felt so miserable. I thought I would never get another chance to translate for Amma. I promised myself if I ever did get another chance, I would never again try to prove that I was right and Amma was wrong. Perhaps detecting my inner resolve, in the next city on that tour, Amma very compassionately called me and asked me to translate.

Hearing this story, one might suggest that Amma has many Tamil devotees and would have had some understanding of the Tamil language, and it is no miracle that Amma was able to correct my words. But Amma can do, and has done, the same thing many times with languages that should be utterly foreign to Her.

The first time Amma went to France, as Her talk was being translated into French, Amma interrupted the translator and repeated one of Her points, asking him to translate that again. When She did this, he realized that he had forgotten to mention that point at all. Even though he was speaking in French, Amma knew that he had missed one particular point. Later he asked Amma, "You don't speak French at all; how did you know I hadn't translated that point?"

Amma replied, "It is true Amma doesn't know the language, but Amma can see your mind. Before the words come out of your mouth, they are in the form of thoughts, aren't they? The subtle form of speech is thought. Amma was watching your thoughts, and She could see that you had left this point out."

A brahmachari working in Amma's Amrita Kuteeram project returned to the ashram from a construction site in Bangalore and asked Amma if he could work in a construction site closer to Amritapuri Ashram, to which Amma agreed. After a week of working in a site close to the ashram, one day Amma called him during the morning darshan and told him that he should immediately leave for another construction site, this one in Ernakulam (about three hours away from the ashram). He was very upset and asked Amma if it was all right if he left after a couple of more weeks, as he had only just come back from Bangalore. Amma insisted that he should leave to Ernakulam immediately. He came to me crying, telling me that he did not want to go. I tried to convince him that a disciple must adhere to the Guru's instructions as closely as possible. Citing some of my own experiences, I finally convinced him to leave. He left in the early evening and went to the construction site in Ernakulam where he made arrangements to take over the construction from another brahmachari. After just one hour he developed an unbearable stomachache and was immediately admitted to AIMS, Amma's super-specialty hospital located just a short drive from the construction site. As his condition worsened, the doctors took an ultrasound and found that the brahmachari's appendix was going to burst any minute. He was rushed to an operating room where his appendix was removed just in time. After being discharged from the hospital, Amma allowed the brahmachari to return to the ashram and, after recuperating, work in one of the construction sites nearby.

When the brahmachari had come to me crying, even as I had done my best to convince him to follow Amma's instructions to a T, I had inwardly wondered why Amma was so keen to send him away again so soon. I thought it was strange that She would not allow him to spend even one more day in the ashram. After hearing about the brahmachari's operation, the motivation for Amma's urgent directive became crystal clear. She had known that he needed to be near the hospital on that very day. If his appendix had flared up at the ashram that night, there would have been no way to get him to a hospital in time to remove it, and his condition might even have been fatal.

We may wonder, if Amma knows everything, why She did not simply tell the boy he would need surgery that evening and send him to the hospital. By sending the boy to the construction site, Amma ensured that he did not have to spend the whole day worrying about the upcoming surgery, and he was also able to learn a valuable lesson about the importance of following the Guru's instructions. At the same time, Amma made sure that he was close to the hospital when he needed to be. Also, out of Her own humility, Amma will never directly reveal Her omniscient nature if it is not absolutely necessary to do so.

However, sometimes Amma's mysterious actions or words almost immediately reveal Her omniscient nature, as in the case above. In other instances, such lessons have taken years, even decades to become clear to us.

In the first few years of the ashram, there were only a handful of brahmacharis around Amma. At that time we were so attached to Amma's physical form that we would follow Her everywhere, even if She did not want to be followed. Sometimes She would try to sneak out of the ashram without our knowledge, but somehow we would always find out where She had gone. On one particular occasion Amma went to meet with a family some distance from the ashram. Amma was sitting in a hut waiting for the family to arrive when the brahmacharis started trickling in one after another and sitting as close to Amma as possible. When the family came, Amma asked us to sit on the other side of the hut.

We followed Am-ma's instructions, but we were not happy about it. After they left, Swami Paramatmananda (then Br. Nealu) told Amma, "Amma, we were very sad when you asked us to move away from you. We did not want to intrude on your discussion with the family; we just wanted to be close to you."

To this, Amma coolly replied, "Now you feel sad when you have to move just two meters away from me. One day you will need binoculars to see me." At the time, we could not understand how Amma's words could come true; we thought She was just using a figure of speech. But more than 20 years later, during *Amritavarsham50—Embracing the World for Peace & Harmony* (Amma's 50th birthday celebration, held as an international peace-prayer event at a stadium in Cochin), when Swami Paramatmananda was trying to make his way to the stage, he was stopped by stadium security guards who did not recognize him as one of Amma's senior disciples. In order to watch the evening program, he was forced to take a seat in the stadium bleachers, from where Amma was just a tiny, sparkling speck of white. It was then that he realized Amma's prophetic words from more than two decades before had come true to the letter.

Sometimes what we learned in the scriptures made Am-ma's task more difficult. I remember when we learned that a True Master can never really be angry with a disciple, and the anger a Master expresses is just a mask put on for the disciple's upliftment.

After we understood this, no matter how much anger Amma showed toward us, we would not take it very seriously. At that time we were so attached to Amma that we wouldn't leave Her alone even for a minute. Amma did not want us to be so attached to Her physical form, so She would try various methods to keep us away: by showing anger, by acting as if She had no love for us.

But nothing would dissuade us from remaining in Her presence and insisting on Her attention.

Sometimes, Amma would lock Herself in the room and wouldn't open the door even if we knocked repeatedly. Once, one of the brahmacharis started calling out, "Ammaa! Ammaa!" outside the door. Then he paused and informed Amma through the door, "Amma, I have called you 10 times." When She didn't respond, he started calling Her name again. Then he stopped and said, "Amma now I have called you 20 times." Then he continued calling Amma and finally he said, "Amma, I have finished the 108 Names now. You have to open the door." Still, Amma did not open the door. Then this brahmachari made noises as if he was crying. Due to Her extremely compassionate nature, Amma was helpless to resist this tactic. Yet when She opened the door, She found the brahmachari standing there smiling.

Sometimes, Amma would sit absorbed in meditation for a long time. At that time we had no clue about the state of *samadhi* (total absorption in the Supreme Self), and we did not have much patience with Amma's withdrawing into Her Self. Sometimes after waiting around for half an hour or so I would go and shake Amma by the shoulder to try to get Her attention. I remember one time when one of the brahmacharis wanted to tell Amma something he considered very important. When Amma did not respond to being called, he went over to Her and slowly but surely began prying open Her eyelids.

Even if Amma pushed us away, we would cling to Her arms, saying, "You can scold us, you can push us away, you can do anything to us. But please don't stay silent, don't be indifferent to us. That is too much for us to bear."

In this we unknowingly gave Amma one of the few keys She had to really discipline us. When She wanted to correct our mistakes, instead of scolding us directly, She would inflict some form of punishment on Her own body. Sometimes She would refuse to eat; other times She would stand waist-deep in a pond for hours on end. This form of education was extremely painful for us, and slowly we learned to take Amma's scoldings more seriously, so She would not have to resort to such drastic measures.

Amma's omniscience was particularly and poignantly evident in Her statements regarding the "coming darkness" in the year 2005. Amma had spoken privately to Her disciples about 2005 for several years. Then in July of 2003, just before a Devi Bhava darshan in Rhode Island, She made a public announcement before a crowd of over 4,000 people. At that time, Amma told everyone not to be afraid but that She felt some bad times were coming. "Amma sees a lot of darkness in the world, and everyone should be extremely careful. When Amma looks down, She sees deep ditches, so unless people are extremely alert, things can become bad."

In fact, this was the main reason Amma agreed to have Her 50th birthday celebrated as an international event in September of 2003. She felt that if hundreds of thousands of people came together to pray for world peace and harmony, it would reduce the effect of whatever calamities were heading our way. Thus started the regular chanting of the peace mantra *Om lokah samastah sukhino bhavantu* (May all the beings in all the worlds be happy)by Amma's children—both individually and collectively—worldwide.

One evening during Amma's 50th birthday celebrations, with more than 200,000 people from all over the world in attendance, Amma asked all Her children to chant the peace mantra for one full minute and to imagine that vibrations of peace were spreading from each of their hearts to the whole planet. When the minute finished, She then asked everyone to take the hands of those sitting next to them and to chant the peace mantra three more times. Amma also conducted a special puja in which She watered a banyan sapling with waters collected from rivers, seas and lakes from almost every nation on earth.

In the summer of 2004, Amma again said She felt that "dark clouds would come and engulf the sky." And when the United Nations asked Her to participate in its International Day of Peace, She gave Her full support, motivating hundreds of thousands to join in a collective prayer for world peace on September 21, 2004. In Her speech that day, Amma said, "Today, the need for prayer and spiritual practices is greater than ever before." Throughout Amma's tour of Europe in October and November 2004, in every city She visited Amma led Her children in collective prayers for peace and harmony in the coming times.

Just a few weeks before the devastating tsunami struck South Asia, Amma told some of Her disciples that She felt the days after Christmas would be very hard times, at one point even saying that the 26th of December would be particularly tragic for many. On the night of the 25th, Amma heard the cawing of crows simultaneously with the call of the nightingale. She became very serious and told Her attendant that it was a very inauspicious omen. That week, Amma was also seen shedding tears while singing bhajans; in particular, a bhajan with the words *lokah samastah sukhino bhavantu*. Seeing Amma crying, many in the ashram also silently shed tears.

Actually, Amma's actions on the day before the tragedy clearly show that She knew something bad was coming. On the 26th of December, 5,000 destitute women from the Alappad district, the coastal area around Amritapuri, were scheduled to collect their free pensions provided quarterly by the ashram. Intuitively, the previous day Amma had sent word ahead that the pension distribution for those ladies should be postponed by one week. Had Amma not done this, the widows would have left their children at home to come and collect their pensions. With no one to rescue them from the rising water, many more children in the village would almost certainly have been killed by the tsunami.

The pension distribution for widows from inland Kollam, on the other hand, was not cancelled, but Amma instructed that it not be done in the bhajan hall—its typical place—but on the jetty on the opposite side of the ashram, right next to the boats to the mainland. Imagine the chaos if that hall, which became completely flooded, had been full of women waiting for their pensions? As it was, the bhajan hall was almost empty when the water came.

Typically, on a Sunday Amma would have been giving darshan in that hall and it would have been packed with at least 15,000 people. However, one hour before the darshan was to begin, Amma said the darshan would be held in the old prayer hall(which is one and a half stories above ground). Because of this, the main hall was nearly empty when the water rushed in.

Even today, if we ask Amma if She is omniscient, She will simply shake Her head and laugh, saying, "I don't know anything. I'm just a crazy girl." A True Master will never boast about his greatness. As Amma says, if we have piled up sugar in a corner, is there any need to write, "This is sugar," on a sign above it? The fact that it is sugar is obvious. If someone stands right next to it and says it is not sugar but salt, is it going to affect the sugar? Such people only miss the opportunity to taste its sweetness, even as a line of people—to whom it is obvious that it is sugar and nothing but sugar—forms right in front of them.

Just before the Mahabharata War began, Lord Krishna made one last effort to avert it. He traveled alone and unarmed as a messenger from the righteous Pandavas into the court of the evil-minded Kauravas. As he issued his plea for peace, Duryodhana, prince of the Kauravas, refused to hear Krishna out and ordered him to be bound and taken away. Having exhausted all other methods, Krishna revealed his *vishwarupa* (cosmic form) to Duryodhana right there in the court.

Even as he gazed at the entire universe revealed within Krishna's form, Duryodhana was not at all impressed. He did not believe his eyes but scoffed at Krishna as a simple magician.

Later, Krishna showed the same cosmic form to Arjuna in the midst of delivering the *Bhagavad Gita* on the battlefield. Arjuna was wonderstruck and fell at Krishna's feet, begging for the Lord's forgiveness for any words he might have spoken casually to Krishna, considering him as his peer. The sight of Krishna's cosmic form both terrified Arjuna and inspired him to take refuge in Krishna alone.

Even when God stands unveiled before us, not everyone will recognize Him. As Christ said, "Those who have eyes to see, let them see."

Chapter 16

The Light of Awareness

Many people have shared with me that after coming to Amma, they feel that they have suddenly developed more negative tendencies and thoughts than they had previously. Thus, the initial inspiration they felt toward doing spiritual practices wanes away. About this, Amma says that actually the negativities were there already. Either we were previously unaware of them, or they were lying dormant in our subconscious mind for want of suitable circumstances in which to arise. Amma tells the following story to illustrate this point.

A man traveling to the Himalayas found a snake lying coiled on the side of the road. Frozen by the snow, it could not even move an inch. Concerned for the snake's welfare, the man started caressing it. It seemed so gentle and harmless that he decided to carry it with him. On his way back, he felt that the snake might be feeling very cold and decided to tuck it under his armpit in order to keep it warm. Slowly, as the snake absorbed the heat from the man's body, it emerged from its hibernation and bit the man with its poisonous fangs.

Likewise, for want of the right situation, our negativities may not manifest immediately. In the presence of a True Master like Amma, the right circumstances to bring even our hibernating vasanas out into the open spontaneously unfold. Only when these negativities are brought into the light of awareness can they be transformed and ultimately transcended.

In Amma's presence, there are so many different circumstances that can bring up our negative feelings such as anger, resentment and jealousy. If we are watching Amma give darshan and someone blocks our view, we may feel angry toward them. If Amma pays more attention to someone else than to us, we may feel jealous toward that person. Someone may ask us not to stand or sit in a particular place. All of these circumstances are opportunities for our negativities to be revealed.

Every year, Amma tours North India for two months. Many people want to accompany Her on these tours, and over the years what began as one or two vans has grown into a huge caravan of six or seven buses as well as a number of smaller vehicles. During one such tour, one of the buses broke down, and the remaining buses had to accommodate the extra passengers. As it was one of the longest rides of the journey and the buses had become somewhat cramped, the additional stress and tension led to arguments breaking out among the passengers. During a short break in the journey, Amma boarded one of the buses and gave a kind of pep talk to everyone. She said that we should remember that whenever a person annoys or criticizes us that it is simply Amma working on us in the form of that person. Later, one passenger sitting on that bus told me that the person sitting behind him had kept repeating the same mistake throughout the tour. Every time he went to take something from his bag on the rack above, he would accidentally drop it on the head of the person who was telling me the story. The other passenger did this over and over, two or three times during any given leg of the journey. The person related to me that he had been able to be loving and kind the first few times, but in the end he had even shouted at the other passenger, "Enough already, you idiot! What is wrong with you?"

But after Amma came on the bus and spoke to everyone, though the other passenger's behavior did not change, this person was able to accept it with a smile.

Sometimes during Amma's afternoon darshan programs, She will ask the line monitors to stop the line for darshan around 5:30 in the afternoon because She has to begin the evening program at 7:30 p.m., and in between She usually has several important meetings scheduled.

The line monitors obediently ask the devotees not to join the line, but they often encounter some resistance. Everyone wants to go for darshan right away, and they all have their excuses. Of course, everybody has their own problems. So it is with great difficulty that the line monitors and sometimes even the brahmacharis and swamis try to help people understand that they can come in the evening, or even the next day if they can't come at night. In many instances they won't listen, however. Instead, they just wait on the sides of the room with long faces. Seeing them standing there, Amma will immediately ask us to open the line to allow 15 more people. Then we will close the line again only to open and close the line three or four more times. Sometimes the devotees get angry with the line monitors. "What are you doing here, asking us to come for darshan but then stopping us?"

In halls where it is set up for the darshan line to come from both sides and for people to exit down the center aisle, Amma does not want people to sit in the center aisle because She wants the space to be free for people to exit. One day Amma mentioned to the line monitors to be sure there was no one in the center aisle for the evening program. When they were setting up in the afternoon, they were careful to make sure that everybody was sitting outside the ropes on either side of the center aisle.

When Amma arrived for the evening program, upon seeing the center line totally empty of people, She asked me, "Why is there such a gap? Make an announcement that anyone can sit there." Everyone was waiting for that opportunity, and the center aisle was full in a matter of moments. The next day, the line monitors decided that since Amma had called everyone to sit in the center aisle the day before, today they would not keep people out of the center aisle. This time, as soon as Amma came, She asked, "Why did you put people in the center aisle? I told you not to put people in the center aisle yesterday; why did you put them there today?"

The line monitors told Amma, "We didn't put anybody there yesterday, but you called everybody so we thought you wanted it that way."

Amma replied, "Just do what I told you to do; don't worry about what I am doing after that."

Through these seemingly contradictory instructions and behaviors, Amma creates situations in which the negative qualities and tendencies of the line monitors will rise up. Through undergoing a series of similar situations, the line monitors have been able to cultivate patience, an attitude of surrender, kindness and other positive mental qualities. In this way, Amma helps them to grow spiritually. The people receiving the contradictory instructions from the line monitors, which they had received from Amma, are also being given similar opportunities to develop positive qualities.

There are many cases of Masters using contradiction as a tool to enlighten the disciple. In fact, this is one of the fundamental tenets of the Zen Buddhist tradition. Zen Masters speak to their disciples in *koans,* or questions with no right answer, in order to trick the disciple into surrendering the intellect and making contact with the Pure Consciousness beyond. For example, the Zen Master Shuzan held out his short staff and said to one of his disciples, "If you call this a short staff, you oppose its Reality. If you do not call it a short staff, you ignore the facts. Now what do you wish to call this?"

One of the best-known examples of this kind of teaching is in the story of Marpa and his favorite disciple, Milarepa. After a troubled childhood and a virulent adolescence driven by the desire for vengeance, Milarepa grew dispassionate toward the world and approached the famous Guru Marpa for spiritual instructions. However, Marpa would not immediately accept him as a disciple. First, he told Milarepa that he would like him to build a stone structure on a high rocky ridge overlooking Marpa's property. Having a great thirst for knowledge of the Truth, Milarepa leapt at the opportunity to serve his Guru. Milarepa had to haul all the boulders and stones on foot from a nearby rock quarry, and there was no one to help him build the tower. It was grueling work, and it took months of intense labor. One day when Milarepa was working on the tower, Marpa came out and inspected his work. After looking at the tower for a few moments, Marpa asked Milarepa to tear it down and take all the rocks and boulders back to where they had been found. Marpa said that he had changed his plans and now wanted a new structure built in another place. This was repeated over and over again until finally he had Milarepa build a grand, nine-storied tower (which remains standing even today). Throughout these arduous, seemingly pointless tasks, Milarepa put forth a Herculean effort and never lost faith that he would receive the instructions he was looking for. He moved stones that ordinarily could only be moved by the combined strength of three men. He put forth such strenuous effort that his back became one great sore from carrying rocks and mortar. His arms and legs were all cracked and bruised. Yet he continued working on, every day hoping at last to be favored with some religious instruction. Out of sympathy, Marpa showed him how to pad his back and allowed him to rest while his body healed, but never did he allow Milarepa to avoid any of the building work that he had set out for him to complete.

Milarepa persevered like this for years. Finally, he gave up hope of ever being accepted as a disciple and left Marpa's ashram, planning never to return. Everyone expected Marpa to be nonchalant about this departure, as he had never shown any obvious affection toward Milarepa. But when Marpa heard the news, he burst into tears, saying, "Bring him back, for heaven's sake! He is my dearest disciple."

When Marpa finally did accept Milarepa as his disciple, he told him that even though he had always loved Milarepa dearly and seen his great potential, as Milarepa had performed so many heinous deeds in his early life, he had no choice but to treat him in this way. Marpa's seemingly contradictory and senseless instructions had only been to help Milarepa break free from the chains of his past actions.

Swami Paramatmananda relates a similar story from his early relationship with Amma. One day Amma decided that it was time to build two huts in addition to the one that we already had. With the influx of permanent residents, some more rooms were needed.

Swami Paramatmananda (then Br. Nealu) was in charge of supervising the work. After designing a plan, he showed it to Amma and got Her approval. The plan consisted of three huts facing away from each other in a U-shape. He thought that this would conserve space and make it possible for the breeze to enter through the doorways of each of the huts.

Privately, he was proud of the plan and the way the work was unfolding.

A few hours after the work had commenced, Amma passed by the work site. Seeing the way in which the huts were being constructed, Amma suddenly exclaimed, "Who told them to build the huts this way?" Everyone pointed at Swami Paramatmananda. He reminded Amma that She had seen the plan and approved of it.

"I don't remember seeing any plan. Tear this down! Nobody should build huts facing away from each other. All you think of is how to be comfortable, how to get a good breeze! Don't you care about traditional rules? The rules do not allow huts to be built like this." So saying, Amma left the work site.

Swami Paramatmananda instructed the workers to tear down the work that they had been doing since morning.

After a short while, Amma returned. Looking at the workers who had started to dismantle the huts, She said, "What are they doing? Tell them to build them the way they originally planned. Otherwise, how is the breeze going to enter the huts?"

"But Amma, what about the traditional rules?" Swami Paramatmananda asked.

"Rules? There are no rules for building huts. That's only for regular buildings."

An onlooker might have thought that Amma was crazy. But Swami Paramatmananda understood that the whole situation was Amma's way of bringing out his pride and helping him overcome it.

The circumstances created by Amma are the best and fastest way to mature our minds. In fact Amma compares Her ashram

to Kurukshetra, the battlefield where, along with their respective armies, the five Pandavas waged war against the 100 Kauravas in the Mahabharata War. Though the Pandavas were on the side of dharma, they were vastly outnumbered by the Kauravas. The Kauravas' army was also much bigger than the army of the Pandavas. And yet, because the Pandavas had Lord Krishna on their side, they were able to prevail over the Kauravas.

This is said to be symbolic of the ratio of positive and negative qualities within most of us. Even though our negativities may seem to be more powerful and many more in number than our good qualities, with the grace of a True Master, we can wage war against our own negative qualities. This is not a battle that must be fought on one occasion and either won or lost; it is a battle we must fight many times each day—in fact, in every moment of our life.

Sometimes, we may be aware of our negative qualities without feeling the need to get rid of them. We have all met someone who seems happy to be depressed, and we have all had the experience of justifying our anger toward someone. Sometimes, after losing our temper with someone, we even feel good about having given them a piece of our mind.

Once a man was driving down a highway when he saw a broken-down truck with a very distraught-looking man puttering around the engine. He decided to pull over and see if he could lend a hand.

"I don't know much about engines," he explained to the stranded truck driver, "but is there some way I can help you?"

"Yes, yes!" the truck driver exclaimed. "You see, I've got two crocodiles in the back of this truck. But they're pretty claustrophobic, and I can't leave them in there for long. Mister, you got to get these crocs to the zoo ASAP!"

"No problem," said the man. The truck driver helped him load the crocodiles into the back seat of his car. They strapped them in as best they could, and the man sped off in the direction of the zoo.

About two hours later, as the truck driver was still stranded by the side of the road, he saw the man speeding by in the other direction with the crocodiles still in the car. This time, one of them was in the passenger seat.

The truck driver managed to flag the man down. "What are you, crazy?! I told you to get those crocodiles to the zoo!"

"We went to the zoo," the man explained enthusiastically. "And we had so much fun, we're going to the movies!"

Similarly, we keep company with our inner enemies like jealousy, anger, pride and lust, not knowing that they can devour us at any moment. In order to overcome our vasanas, we need to be able to see the harmful effects they have on us and others. Even if we are comfortable with our vasanas, we can be sure that others are not.

One day a neighbor called on Mullah Nasruddin and asked to borrow the Mullah's donkey.

"I'm sorry," the Mullah said, "but I've already lent it out." No sooner had he spoken than the sound of a donkey braying came from the Mullah's stable.

"But Mullah, I can hear your donkey in there."

"Shame on you," the Mullah protested indignantly, "that you would take the word of a donkey over my own!"

Like this, even when others point out that we are wrong, we stubbornly cling to our own view and find ways to justify it.

Amma says that one may sit in a cave and meditate for long hours each day, but when one comes out of the cave, one may lose one's temper or feel disgusted or jealous toward another person, and when one reacts in this way, much of the spiritual energy one has accumulated is dissipated needlessly. Amma often gives the example of the Sage Vishwamitra who did penance for thousands of years. However, he was very hot-tempered, and whenever he emerged from meditation, he would lose his temper very easily. In order to regain the energy he had lost, he would have to sit for many more years. Finally he did achieve Self-realization, but it took much longer than it might have if he had been able to overcome his habit of losing his temper earlier.

That is why Amma places so much emphasis on helping and working with others in addition to meditation and other more personal spiritual practices. When we live and work in concert with others, we are able to uncover and overcome negative tendencies of which we might otherwise have never even been aware.

There is a joke about a conversation between two monks from different traditions. One monk asked the other, "What is your spiritual discipline?"

"Oh, I have a very strict discipline. I wake up at two in the morning every day and chant and pray until breakfast. Actually, on many days I don't even eat breakfast. I fast more than 100 days each year. And it is only because you are talking to me today that I can even speak to you. Most days, I am observing a vow of silence, and I am in solitude as well."

"Oh, that is a very strict discipline…" the first monk commented.

"Why do you say that?" the second monk asked. "Surely you must be doing nearly the same."

"Not really," the first monk confessed ruefully.

"What do you do then?" the second monk inquired.

"I live in a community along with 100 other monks," the first monk said simply.

On hearing this, the second monk said, "I bow down to you, Brother. Your discipline is far greater than mine."

Even though the second monk performed a great deal more austerities, he considered the first monk's renunciation to be greater than his own, simply because he was able to live and work closely with other monks.

In the Ayurvedic system of healthcare, medicine is considered only 50 percent of the treatment. The other half of treatment is called *pathyam*. This refers to the disciplines we need to follow with regard to diet, rest, bathing, etc. Only if we follow these disciplines will the medicine be effective. In the same way, spiritual practices are only 50 percent of spirituality. The rest lies in overcoming the negativities in our own mind and in how we respond to the various situations of life.

Amma says, "It is important to recognize and accept whatever you are—whether you are ignorant, illiterate, knowledgeable, ethical or egoistic." In order to make real progress, we will have to start by looking honestly at ourselves and our faults.

The famous jazz musician Rafi Zabor once said, "God speaks as softly as He can, and as loudly as He has to." One way or another, it is the Guru's task to help us overcome our shortcomings. Sometimes—whenever possible—the Guru will do this gently. But at times, the Guru will have to take seemingly drastic measures to help us see and overcome our drawbacks. Amma tells the following story to illustrate this point.

Once a Guru and his disciple were returning to their ashram after visiting a village. It was a long walk, and they had been traveling for many hours. As they were traveling through a cool, shady forest, the disciple, who had been suffering in silence for a long time and could not resist any longer, finally asked his Master if they couldn't just lie down and rest for a while. The Guru gently suggested that it would be better if they continued on, but the disciple pressed his point and the Guru relented. Some time later, when the Guru stood up again, the disciple, who had by now fully given in to his exhaustion, moaned loudly, "I cannot move even another inch! Master, I don't want to keep you from the ashram, but at least let me rest here in this nice shady forest until tomorrow." The Guru agreed and continued on by himself. Once out of the forest, he happened upon a family of farmers who were tending their field. The Guru suddenly picked up one of the family's children and ran back into the forest in the direction he had come, cradling the child under his arm. Behind him went up a hue and cry as the family realized their darling daughter had been kidnapped. They sent word for all the neighbors to join them in their attempt to rescue her.

When the sprinting Guru reached his disciple, who was by now sleeping deeply, he set the child gently down on the ground and asked her to sit there next to the disciple. The child happily obeyed, and the Guru disappeared.

Thus it was that the angry search party came upon the sleeping disciple with the lost child seated next to him. Of course they assumed that the disciple was the kidnapper and wasted no time in waking him up. As they began to rain blows upon him, the disciple rolled away from them and sprung to his feet, racing away from the search party and toward the safety of his ashram. And so the disciple, who had so recently been declaring that he could not move another inch, reached the ashram even before the Guru.

This was a case of the Guru trying to correct the disciple gently, but when this did not work, he had to resort to tougher methods.

Even after I joined the ashram, according to Amma's instructions, I continued to work in a bank for several years. All the other brahmacharis had started taking scriptural classes, but as the classes took place during working hours, I was not able to attend. When I came back to the ashram from work, I would look through their notes and try to absorb as much as I could.

One day, one of my spiritual brothers was advising me about how to behave in front of the Guru. He told me that one should be careful even of one's body language: not to stand proudly; not to look straight into the eyes of the Guru; to always speak in a soft tone, etc. He explained to me that even if the Guru falsely accuses you of making a mistake, you should never protest or make excuses, understanding that this is only the Guru's way of highlighting your negative tendencies.

As he had already started studying the scriptures, I was listening with rapt attention to what he was saying. At that moment, Amma suddenly called him into Her room. He left me standing there and went running to Amma's room. A few minutes later, I could hear both Amma's voice and the voice of the brahmachari who had so recently been advising me in the proper way to conduct oneself in the presence of the Guru. However, the brahmachari's voice was much louder than Amma's. When I ran to the room to find out what was happening, I found the brahmachari arguing vehemently against something Amma was saying to him. When he saw me standing there, he must have recalled his earlier advice to me as he sheepishly lowered his voice and softened his tone. He instantly realized that Amma had only created the situation to see whether he could practice what he had been preaching.

In January of 2003, the ashram completed a housing colony of 108 homes in Rameshwaram, Tamil Nadu, and distributed the homes to local homeless families. Later, as Rameshwaram was his native place, the President of India, Dr. A.P.J. Abdul Kalam, visited the housing colony. Impressed with the work, the president decided to donate 10 months of his presidential salary to Amma's ashram. That money was used to help the ashram construct a surgical ward in Rameshwaram as an adjunct to the government hospital. As the surgical ward was nearing completion, and before it was turned over to the government hospital as planned, a brahmachari who was posted at Rameshwaram informed Amma that the president was scheduled to visit again soon. Amma received this news while She was giving darshan and suggested to a devotee seated nearby that as long as the president was in Rameshwaram, he could be invited to inaugurate the new surgical ward. The devotee immediately got up to try to reach the office of the president.

Fortunately the president's secretary was in the office when the devotee called. As the president had met Amma previously on several occasions, the president's secretary told the devotee that he would definitely convey the invitation to the president. Less than half an hour later, the secretary called the devotee back and said that the president had graciously agreed to briefly visit and inaugurate the surgical ward on the day of his visit to Rameshwaram.

The devotee was ecstatic, thinking that Amma was sure to be pleased with him for having arranged everything so quickly.

He rushed back to the darshan hall to inform Amma of his achievement. However, when he reached Amma's side, he found that Amma would not even look at him. It was not that She was in a hurry to finish the darshan; in fact, She was spending a lot of time talking to each devotee who came for darshan and also laughing and joking with the other brahmacharis and devotees nearby. However, She kept avoiding the gaze of this particular devotee. It was as if he was invisible. The devotee was astonished, thinking that Amma should be eager to hear the results of his extremely important assignment. After nearly an hour of standing silently, the devotee could not hold back any longer. He told Amma, "The president has agreed to inaugurate the surgical ward. Can you believe I arranged everything in less than an hour?"

Amma told the devotee, "Don't think that you have done anything special. Everything fell into place because of God's grace alone."

Upon hearing Amma's words the devotee was instantly humbled. He realized that even before asking him to perform the task, Amma knew what the result would be, and it was only to give him a chance to perform selfless service—and to learn a valuable lesson—that She had asked him to do it.

Amma is an embodiment of humility, but She will only act humble as long as it serves to increase our own humility. If Her humility is only going to increase our own ego, then She will have to assume the role of a teacher and directly point out our mistakes.

In the early years of the ashram, we had a very small septic tank that needed to be emptied out manually. On certain festival days, the septic tank would be filled to the point of overflowing. On such occasions, everyone held their nose when they passed by and remarked about the disgusting smell, but no one was ready to do the work of emptying out the septic tank.

Once, on the day after such a festival, when all the devotees had left and only a few brahmacharis remained, we were getting ready for bhajans. Usually, Amma would never miss the evening bhajans. But on that particular day, when it was time for the bhajans to begin, Amma had not arrived. Remaining faithful to the ashram discipline, one of the brahmacharis started singing, and we all joined him. But after one song and then another was completed, we started to wonder what was happening. One of us got up and went to Amma's room, but he returned reporting that She was not there either. Finally someone discovered Amma standing in the overflow area of the septic tank, trying to lift the cement slab off the top of the tank. This person ran to inform us of what Amma was doing. By the time we reached there, She had already succeeded in removing the lid and was scooping out the waste, one bucket at a time.

We felt terrible seeing Amma standing there doing the work which we had all been loathe to do, and we knew that the proper thing to do would be to jump in and help Her. However, we were still reluctant to do so, and Amma did not ask us to. Finally, one brahmachari stepped inside the tank and began helping Amma clean out the tank. A couple of us had the bright idea of standing outside the tank and carrying the buckets from the tank to the backwaters to avoid having to step inside the tank. Because they had taken that job, the rest of us had no other choice than to get into the tank. As we carried out the work, Amma and all the rest of us were covered in waste, but seeing Amma's attitude of blissful indifference—She could just as easily have been bailing out pure water—we gradually lost our disgust toward the work we were doing.

After that, whenever the septic tank was full, the brahmacharis would clean it out without even being asked. And Amma was always there alongside us.

The valuable lessons gleaned from such experiences have stayed with me even up to the present day. On the last day of *Amritavarsham50*, the four-day celebration of Amma's 50th birthday, I was given the responsibility of welcoming and introducing the president of India to the hundreds of thousands of devotees and admirers of Amma gathered in the stadium.

Later that day, I was in Amma's car on the way back to the ashram. I was very happy that the celebrations had been so successful. I was not feeling proud, exactly... if there was any feeling of pride it was for Amma and the entire ashram, rather than myself. I was just marveling at the magnitude of the whole affair, as well as feeling pretty good about having had the privilege of introducing the President of India. On the way back to the ashram, Amma gave me my next assignment. She commented that more than 50 schools in Cochin had been used to accommodate devotees who were attending the celebrations, and now that the schools were to be turned back over to the students, we should be very sure that the schools had been cleaned properly. Specifically, Amma said that the bathrooms and toilets in the schools, which had been used by thousands of people over the past four days, should be spic and span. And, She wanted me to personally oversee the cleaning work. So saying, She stopped the car halfway to the ashram and asked me to get out and go back to Cochin immediately.

Hearing Amma's instructions, I was sure that She must have detected the "good" feeling I had from having introduced the president and wanted to be sure that I did not develop any feelings of pride or egoism. Thus I went from introducing the president on one day to cleaning dozens of filthy toilets the next. If the same thing had happened to me years ago, I would have felt terrible about it. But now I was able to draw inspiration not only from Amma's earlier example of having cleaned the septic tank but even more so from Amma's very recent example in Amritapuri.

In the days before the *Amritavarsham50* celebrations began, there was a seemingly unending stream of dignitaries wanting to meet privately with Amma. One morning, immediately after Amma finished meeting with several government ministers and other dignitaries, She walked down the steps from Her room and began helping some devotees stitch woven plastic sacks together in order to make curtains for the hundreds of public toilets that the ashram was building in and around the stadium and at the schools and other accommodation sites where the devotees attending the celebrations would be staying. Even having known Amma for so many years, I was amazed at the sight. Having just met so many important officials and CEOs, Amma did not hesitate to do the most menial labor. Though I already knew that Amma never misses even a seemingly minor detail, and She never considers any work beneath Her, She never ceases to surprise me with the depth of Her humility and expansiveness of Her vision. To me, it was one thing for Amma to be ready to clean the septic tank when this was just a humble hermitage with only a few brahmacharis living in huts, and quite another for Amma to still be ready to do the same type of work when there were so many dignitaries lining up to meet Her. But to Amma, it was the same.

Amma's greatest teaching has always been the example of Her own actions. One of the most dramatic examples I have seen Her set thus far was on the last day of *Amritavarsham50*. Amma joined Her children in the *Amritavarsham50* stadium on September 27th at 9:30 a.m. After an award ceremony, some speeches and cultural programs, She began giving darshan. It wasn't until 8:00 a.m. the next morning that Amma left the stage–almost 24 hours later, 19 of it spent in giving darshan without a break. Even though it was Amma's birthday, it was She who gave the most–the supreme gift of Herself.

When Amma finally stood up after that marathon darshan session, there was a beautiful silence. She looked around the stadium at the thousands upon thousands of Her children who still surrounded Her. She raised Her hands in one last *pranam* (palms joined in reverence). Many people expected Her to collapse with exhaustion. On the contrary, Amma accepted a new pair of *kaimanis* (hand cymbals) someone handed to Her and chimed out a simple, joyful rhythm—as if keeping the beat for dancers only She could see—as She walked off the stage with a relaxed, blissful smile on Her face. *Amritavarsham50* was over.

Chapter 17

Grace Flows Toward Innocent Hearts

There was a poor, elderly devotee from Tamil Nadu who used to do seva in the gardens of Amma's Amrita Vidyalayam (primary school) in Chennai. Even though he was very poor, he would never accept any money for his services. One day a relative presented him with two new white button-down shirts and two white dhotis. Since his old clothes were very worn, the devotee decided to accept one set for himself, but the other set he kept aside, as was his practice, in his puja room in front of Amma's photo, waiting for the day when he could see Amma and offer it to Her.

Finally, almost a year later, the devotee had an opportunity to visit Amritapuri. He brought the new set of clothing with him. As he approached Amma in the darshan line, he began to feel nervous about offering the clothing to Amma. It was a man's set of clothing, after all.

When he reached Amma, he hesitantly offered it to Her. Amma opened the package and found the new white shirt and dhoti inside. To everyone's great surprise, instead of blessing the clothes and passing them on to a nearby attendant, Amma immediately put the shirt on over Her sari and continued giving darshan. Amma wore the man's shirt over Her sari for hours. Later,

Amma said that seeing his innocence, She spontaneously decided to wear the shirt. The man's eyes welled up with tears, so moved was he by Amma's spontaneous gesture of appreciation for his gift. Amma asked those sitting near Her to make space for him, and he sat next to Amma for a long time. Seeing this incident, I was reminded of a similar story from the life of Lord Krishna.

There was a great but very poor devotee of Lord Krishna named Kuchela who had been a childhood friend of the Lord. One day Kuchela's wife felt that she could no longer bear the financial strain they were under, and she suggested Kuchela go see Lord Krishna, who was by now a king, and ask him for his help. Kuchela was appalled at the idea, saying that Krishna was the Lord Himself, and he could not imagine asking the Lord for anything but more devotion. However, his wife continued pressing the idea for days and weeks, and finally, in order to save the children from starvation, Kuchela agreed at least to go and see the Lord, though he was still not ready to ask the Lord for anything. He told his wife not to get her hopes up, as it was very likely that Lord Krishna would not recognize him or invite him in. Also, though he did not have anything substantial to offer Him, he insisted that he could not go to the Lord empty-handed. Kuchela's wife reminded him that as a child, Krishna's favorite snack had been *avil*, or flattened rice. Before Kuchela went to see Lord Krishna, his wife prepared a handful of flattened rice for him to offer to the Lord.

As Kuchela was leaving the house, his wife brought the flattened rice to him. She did not have anything in which to wrap it, so she tied it into a corner of Kuchela's shawl. It took Kuchela several days to walk to Krishna's palace, and his anxiety increased with every passing hour. He was sure that he would not be admitted to the palace.

However, Krishna happened to see Kuchela from the palace and went running down to the front gate to receive his old childhood friend and great devotee. Krishna welcomed him in with overwhelming joy and even knelt and washed the feet of Kuchela who had walked so many days to pay homage to Him. Kuchela cringed at the sight of this; he couldn't bear to allow his beloved Lord to wash his feet, but Krishna insisted.

Then the Lord escorted him into the palace and offered him a seat, all the while reminding him of the happy days they had spent together in school at their Guru's feet. The longer Krishna spoke, and the more Kuchela took in of the Lord's palatial surroundings, the more he felt that he could not possibly present his simple offering of flattened rice to the Lord. Yet even while Kuchela was trying to hide the offering tied in the corner of his tattered shawl, Krishna reached for it and untied it and, catching the flattened rice in his hand, began to eat it with great relish. Kuchela's innocent devotion had made the simple offering of flattened rice delicious to the Lord.

Kuchela left Dwaraka overjoyed at having received the Lord's darshan and so much of His kindness and affection, but as he neared home he began to feel sad, remembering his family and the starving children. He was afraid of what his wife would say when she found out that he had not asked Krishna for anything.

Lost in thought, he passed his own house without noticing that it had undergone a great transformation. Overnight, his simple hovel had become a sparkling mansion. His wife saw him pass by and called him back, relating how suddenly happiness and prosperity had been showered upon them by Krishna's grace.

According to the tradition of Sanatana Dharma, it is not so much the external worship that is important as it is the innocence and love with which the worship is performed. Of course, the rites and rituals can help to cultivate devotion and concentration in our minds. But a stone or a blade of grass offered with a heart full of love and devotion is more precious to the Lord than the most elaborate yagna performed with a heart full of pride and ego.

In the *Bhagavad Gita*, Lord Krishna says,

patraṁ puṣpaṁ phalaṁ toyaṁ yo me bhaktyā prayacchati
tad ahaṁ bhakty upahṛtam aśnāmi prayatātmanaḥ

Whoever offers Me with devotion, a leaf, a flower, a fruit or water, I accept that, the pious offering of the pure in heart.

(IX.26)

On one of Amma's recent European tours, a devotee from Hawaii purchased a garland to offer to Amma. Due to time constraints, she was not able to get darshan that afternoon; she was asked to come back and receive Amma's darshan that evening. This meant that she had to carry the garland with her for several hours before she could offer it to Amma. Perhaps due to her own cultural background, and because she did not know that such a thing was inappropriate according to Indian custom, she put the garland around her own neck and wore it until it was time to receive Amma's darshan. I happened to be standing near Amma when she came for darshan. As the lady was moving forward in the darshan line, I noticed that she was wearing the garland, which had by then become wilted. When it was almost her turn for darshan, she removed the garland and as she was about to put it around Amma's neck, I tried to catch it and prevent her from doing so. I informed her that it was not right to offer something to Amma after we ourselves have worn it. I suggested that she bring a fresh one, and she could garland Amma with that. Amma pushed my arm away and insisted that the lady be allowed to garland Amma with the one she had been wearing. The lady tearfully explained that she had only been wearing the garland around her neck to keep it safely until she had the chance to offer it to Amma. Where I could see only that the lady was not following the proper tradition and inadvertently showing disrespect toward Amma, Amma saw only the lady's innocent desire to garland Her.

This incident reminded me of the story of the Indian saint Andal, who was the adopted daughter of a great devotee named Vishnu Chittar, or "one whose mind is immersed in Vishnu." Vishnu Chittar's primary spiritual practice was to make a garland by hand for the Vishnu *murti* (stone idol representing a particular deity) in a nearby temple. One day as Vishnu Chittar was out in his garden plucking *tulasi* (holy basil) leaves for the day's flower garland, he discovered a baby girl lying on the bare earth. Thinking someone had left the baby by accident, he searched the entire neighborhood for her parents. As no one had heard a word about the child, he decided that she was a gift from his beloved Lord Vishnu and raised the girl as his own child with tremendous love and affection.

As she grew, Vishnu Chittar would regale his daughter Andal with the stories of Lord Krishna's childhood pranks and his lilas with the gopis. Soon Vishnu Chittar found that his daughter was losing her heart to the most charming of all *Avatars* (Divine Incarnations), the cowherd boy of Brindavan. While Vishnu Chittar felt the Lord to be his own dear son, Andal related to the Lord as her beloved sweetheart. As she got older, this feeling deepened within her. Even as a teenager, she did not show any interest in boys but only thought of Her beloved Lord Krishna.

All those years, Vishnu Chittar kept up his habit of making a garland for the Vishnu murti. It was his custom to make the garland in the early morning and then leave the garland in his puja room while he went down to the nearby river for a bath before taking the garland to the temple. What he did not know was that Andal had developed a custom of her own, which was to wait until Vishnu Chittar had gone down to the river and then to take the garland he had made and put it around her own neck. She did this in perfect innocence, looking in the mirror and wondering how it would fit her Lord.

One day after returning from his morning bath, Vishnu Chittar picked up the garland from his altar and discovered a long black hair stuck in it. As he was sure it was not his own hair, he had no idea how it could have happened. Feeling it would be impossible to offer such a garland to the murti, he did not visit the temple that day. The next morning he woke up still very disturbed by the incident of the previous day, and though he made a garland as usual in the early hours of the day and left it on his altar, here he broke with his custom. Instead of going down to the river for a bath, he hid near the puja room, hoping to discover the culprit. To his great surprise, he saw his daughter taking the garland and putting it around her own neck, admiring her reflection and blissfully ignorant of the world outside. Enraged and appalled that his own daughter had committed sacrilege against his beloved Lord, he burst into the puja room and snatched the garland away from the distraught Andal. That day also, he did not offer a garland to the deity. He resolved to make his most beautiful garland ever the following day and to ensure that his blasphemous daughter would not get anywhere near it. That night, he had a divine vision of Lord Vishnu who informed him that He did not want any garland from Vishnu Chittar unless

His dear Andal had worn it first. It was only then that Vishnu Chittar realized the greatness of his daughter's devotion. Though what she was doing was not according to the prescribed tradition, her innocent love for the Lord and one-pointed devotion toward Him alone had made Andal very dear to His heart.

These stories of devotion, both ancient and modern, show us that above all, an innocent heart is what is needed to attract the grace of God. Even if we memorize the most complicated of rituals and texts, without an innocent love for God, it will be difficult to make any real spiritual progress.

One of Amma's brahmacharis shared with me a touching story. A very poor lady with tears dripping from her eyes came for Amma's darshan at Amritapuri. When Amma asked her why she was crying, she said, "I can't find my sandals, Amma."

Hearing this the brahmachari was slightly irritated, thinking, "Asking Amma for a pair of sandals is like asking a benevolent king for a carrot."

And yet, Amma took the lady's concern very seriously, saying it was because of the carelessness of the ashram residents that this poor lady lost her sandals. "People living in the ashram are not aware of the difficulties of worldly life," Amma commented. "These people undergo so much trauma and agony in their lives. They are striving so hard just to get regular meals, just to make ends meet. And it is through that hard-earned money that they have to buy their sandals."

Another brahmachari nearby explained to Amma that some of the devotees were not using the footwear stalls provided at the ashram but rather leaving their sandals under the staircase leading to the darshan hall; as many people's sandals look alike, the occasional disappearance was unavoidable.

Amma was not dissuaded so easily. She instructed the brahmachari to provide plastic bags in which the devotees could bring their sandals along with them when they came for Amma's darshan.

Still, some of the brahmacharis standing nearby objected, saying, "Amma, it is not proper to bring sandals when approaching a Master."

"Do you think that sandals are something so low?" Amma asked incredulously. "In God's creation there is nothing that is low. Amma sees these sandals as a form of God, as they protect the feet of Amma's children from stones and thorns. You are trying to see Brahman everywhere, yet you cannot even accept a pair of sandals as divine." So saying, Amma asked a brahmachari to give the poor lady a new pair of sandals.

We find a very similar story in the life of Lord Krishna. At the beginning of the Mahabharata War, Bhishma, who was the general of the Kauravas' army, was wreaking havoc in the army of the Pandavas. In the face of this onslaught, the morale of the Pandavas' army was fading fast, and finally Krishna decided to go and see Bhishma, who was also his devotee, in the enemy camp of the Kauravas. Draupadi, the wife of all five of the Pandava brothers[2], accompanied Krishna on this midnight mission.

---

[2] To readers unfamiliar with the epic *Mahabharata*, it may seem strange to hear that a noble woman like Draupadi married five righteous men like the Pandavas. But this relationship is very symbolic on a number of levels. Taken at the level of the story, the Pandavas all married Draupadi because of their devotion and respect for their mother and her instructions. Arjuna won the right to marry Draupadi in an archery competition. After the marriage, the five brothers brought Draupadi home with them to introduce her to their mother. In their eagerness, they did not even wait to get inside to share the good news. As they approached their home, they shouted, "Dear mother, look what we have brought home with us!"

Upon reaching Bhishma's tent, the Lord quietly explained to Draupadi that Bhishma was sleeping, and she should go inside and prostrate to him. Draupadi removed her sandals and went inside, following Krishna's instructions.

As she entered, Bhishma stirred, and when he noticed that a lady was prostrating to him, he uttered the boon, "May you remain happily married." When Draupadi stood up and he realized that he had just blessed the wife of his enemies, he flew into a rage, saying, "How dare you come here!? Who accompanied you?" Throwing open the door of the tent, he saw his beloved Lord Krishna holding Draupadi's sandals in his hand. After Draupadi had entered the tent, it had begun to rain, and Krishna was now soaking wet.

Bhishma was shocked at the sight of Krishna standing in the rain, even more so with the sandals in his hands. "My dearest Lord!" he exclaimed. "What is this?"

The Lord smiled sweetly. "The rain started suddenly. As I was afraid that Draupadi's sandals would get wet, I tried to cover them with my shawl."

Without looking, and assuming her sons were referring to an object of some kind, the Pandavas' mother called out, "Whatever it is, share it between the five of you as you have always done."

The Pandavas were shocked to hear this instruction, but as it was coming from their mother, they felt they had no choice but to obey it, and each one married the same woman.

Symbolically, each of the Pandavas represents a different characteristic of a noble human being. Sahadev represents devotion and intelligence; Nakula represents physical beauty; Yudhishthira was the embodiment of dharma; Arjuna symbolizes courage; and Bhima represents physical strength. Taken in this way, Draupadi's marriage to the five Pandavas is meant to show the importance of cultivating each of these qualities in our own character.

Realizing what had happened, Draupadi cried in a panicked tone, "My Lord! Tomorrow the world may decry you, that you held the footwear of a lady!"

Krishna calmly replied, "Let the world realize that my devotees' footwear is precious indeed. God resides in each and every object. These sandals are an image of the Lord."

Amma says the Guru lives for the disciple, for the devotee. Keeping this statement in mind, it is easy to see how our beloved Amma and Lord Krishna could place so much importance on the footwear of their devotees. After all, if we lose our own shoes, don't we get upset? I have often seen people at Amma's programs searching for their lost shoes as if their lives depended on it. And yet, we are not able to place much importance on the same item if it belongs to others. But even if we are not able to see God in sandals, at least let us love the devotees who wear them, remembering that God is residing in each and every one.

Chapter 18

The Mystery of Grace

A man dies and finds himself at the gates of heaven. St. Peter tells the man, "You need 100 points to gain entry into heaven. Now, tell me all the good things you've done, and I'll give you a certain number of points for each item, depending on how good it was. When you reach 100 points, you get in."

"Okay," the man says, "I was married to the same woman for 50 years and never cheated on her. I never even looked at another woman with desire in my heart."

"That's great," says St. Peter. "That's worth two points!"

"Two points?" says the man, sounding a little discouraged. "Well, I went church every Sunday of my life and directed the church choir. I also volunteered my time there in other ways and gave regular donations."

"Good for you," says St. Peter. "That's certainly worth a point."

"One point? How about this: I worked as a charitable doctor, visiting war-torn areas and administering aid to those in need. Plus, I adopted and raised three crippled orphans from the foreign lands I visited."

"Terrific, that's good for two more points," he says.

"Two points!?" The man throws up his hands. "At this rate, the only way I can get into heaven is by the grace of God!"

"Exactly," St. Peter says.

Amma says that for our efforts to be successful in any field, we need God's grace. Even to cross a street safely, we need grace. In any situation or endeavor, there are so many factors beyond our control. Of course, we can control how much effort we put forth and the attention and care with which we perform our actions. But it is grace that brings all other factors together in a favorable way, resulting in the success of our efforts.

In the summer of 2004, during a morning darshan in Amma's San Ramon Ashram, I was in the darshan hall talking to a devotee. I was holding the initial material I had assembled for my second book, *Ultimate Success*. Talking to the devotee as I went, I slowly made my way to the stage. As I reached the stage, Amma suddenly called me. As soon as I went near Her, She grabbed the small bundle of papers I was holding in my hand. In a loud voice She started making fun of me, telling everyone around that it's always my habit to carry a doggie bag or some papers with me. Saying so, She started going through the papers that She had grabbed from my hand and asked me what it was. I told Amma what it was. Amma immediately exclaimed, "Oh, you are writing a second book!"

"Yes, Amma," I said. "Should I not?"

Amma replied, "Yes, yes, you write it." Saying this She closed Her eyes for a few seconds and showered a wonderful blessing holding the papers in Her hands. If the readers of *Ultimate Success* found anything useful or beneficial therein, it was purely Amma's grace.

We never know how and when divine blessings will come to us. Many years back, when there were only a few people living at the ashram, the swamis began to compose bhajans, which we would sing every night at dusk with Amma. At that time, most of the senior swamis except myself had composed songs. I do not consider myself a great musician, so it had never occurred to me to compose a bhajan. Late one night, however, both lyrics and a tune entered my mind, and I decided to write my first song for Amma. Around one in the morning, I had almost completed the bhajan when I heard a knock at my door. I opened the door and was very surprised to see Amma standing in the doorway. "What are you doing up this late?" Amma innocently inquired.

I explained a little sheepishly that I was composing a bhajan for Amma.

"Oh, just the other day Amma was thinking that most of the other swamis had composed bhajans. Amma was wondering why you have not yet done so." Amma's remark was apparently a casual one, but from it I understood that Amma had planted both the words and the tune for the song in my mind, and I found myself literally an instrument in Her hands.

One of the organizers of Amma's programs in New Mexico relates a beautiful anecdote. The first time Amma visited New Mexico, he picked Amma up at the airport and drove Her to his house. It was raining as they stepped out of the airport. Before getting into the car, Amma stood for some time with Her palm upturned, collecting raindrops in Her hand. Then She turned to this devotee and said, "Grace is always falling like rain. We just have to become open to receive it."

By being open to receive it, Amma does not mean just a simple willingness to receive God's help to be successful. Amma's statement was actually a very scientific one. Amma tells us that each one of us has a subtle aura, and in this aura is recorded a subtle impression of every one of our thoughts, words and actions. In a person who thinks only pure thoughts, speaks only good words, and performs only good actions, the aura will be golden in color and extremely receptive to grace. Whereas, in a person whose mind is full of negative thoughts, such as judgmental, vengeful, jealous or lustful thoughts, who is sharp-tongued and mean-spirited, and whose actions benefit only himself or herself, the aura will be dark and clouded—thus, the light of grace will not be able to pass through. It is the impressions left by this person's own actions that block the flow of grace from reaching him or her.

Only human beings are capable of working to become more receptive to grace. That is why it is said that a human life is a blessed life. All other forms of life lack the discriminative power of human beings—they have no sense of right and wrong or good versus bad. When a dog bites a postal worker for no reason, it is not going to increase or decrease the dog's receptivity to grace, as it is devoid of discrimination. But if a postal worker kicks the dog for no reason, the action will leave a corresponding negative impression on his or her aura; he or she is endowed with discrimination and is supposed to have a sense of dharma. This does not mean that we should feel discouraged, thinking about our previous actions that might have blocked grace from reaching us. Instead, let us rejoice in the possibility of putting forth positive effort in the present moment, which will make us more and more receptive to the flow of grace until our whole life becomes a blessing.

One way to become more receptive to grace is by sincerely following the instructions of a True Master. Once Amma asked the ashram residents to see who could chant the most mantras without interruption. It was not a competition but a challenge to each individual. She instructed us not to chant very fast, as if it were a race, but to chant at a consistent, reasonable speed, with love and attention. Some residents chanted 5,000 mantras, some chanted less, and some chanted more. But finally, as the night wore on, we all went to bed. That is, all but one. One of the ashram residents remained awake for 24 hours, chanting his mantra the entire time. Afterward, Amma gave him two candies as prasad. Does it sound like an insufficient reward? One might suggest that it is only two candies for 24 hours of work, but in fact it was much more than that. It is not the candy that is important but Amma's appreciation. Everyone chanted for a long time, but it didn't occur to anyone else to forgo even sleep in following Amma's instruction. But this one person thought, "Amma said try to chant as many mantras as possible, and since it is possible to go one night without sleeping, let me do it." It was for this thought, this level of dedication, that Amma showed Her appreciation. And whether we know it or not, it is this appreciation—not just anyone's appreciation, but the appreciation of a True Master—that everyone is looking for. If the Guru appreciates us, it means that his grace is flowing toward us.

Of course, Amma will not reject even the worst criminal, but by performing good actions we can become more receptive to Her blessings and grace. Amma often tells the story of a small boy who unknowingly made himself a magnet for Amma's grace and affection. One day while Amma was giving darshan in Amritapuri, someone fell sick and vomited in the middle of the darshan line. The person excused himself to go to the ashram's hospital, but he was in no condition to clean up the vomit in the temple. Yet, those nearby felt that as they did not know the man and it was not their vomit, it was not their duty to clean it up either. Gradually the original witnesses went for darshan and left, yet the vomit remained in the middle of the temple floor, halfway down the darshan line. Each person coming for Amma's darshan had to step over it, and many held their nose and even criticized the ashram, saying there was no one to properly keep it clean. Some told Amma about the mess, but no one volunteered to remove it. Then a small boy, no more than eight or nine years old, reached the point where he would have had to step over it to move forward in the darshan line. Instead of holding his nose and jumping forward, he turned and rushed out of the temple, only to appear a few moments later with a cloth in one hand and a bucket of water in the other. Without looking right or left, the boy knelt down and began to meticulously clean up the other person's vomit. He ran in and out of the temple several times in order to rinse the cloth clean before wiping the floor dry, leaving only a polished, squeaky-clean square of tile where the vomit had been just a few minutes before. Finally the boy went to wash his hands before rejoining the darshan line.

Amma had watched all of this unfold, and when the boy reached Her lap She showered Her love and affection on him. Even after She left the darshan hall and went to Her room, though She was engaged in many meetings and phone calls throughout the day, Amma said that the boy's face kept cropping up in Her mind. About this boy, Amma said that though Her grace flows like a river toward one and all, it was as if by his innocent and purely selfless action, he had dug a small niche in the bank of the river of Her grace, into which it flowed directly and spontaneously.

There are those who feel that they do not need a Guru or even God, and that through their own efforts they will be able to achieve the Supreme Realization. But both the scriptures and the Masters say that our own efforts are limited, and that grace alone can take us across the threshold into final Liberation. As a comparison, Amma says that we can go up to the last stop in a bus, and then it is only a short distance from there to our destination. That final distance can only be traversed with the Guru's grace or God's grace. Amma tells the following story.

There was a *dharmashala* (pilgrims' inn) where food was served to the pilgrims everyday. The rule of the place was that the pilgrims had to ring a bell which was hanging down from the awning, and on hearing the sound, the innkeeper would open the gates and food would be served. One day, a poor little boy who lived on alms arrived at this dharmashala and was trying to ring the bell. The bell was too high for him. He tried to ring the bell with a long stick but still, it was out of his reach. He tried climbing on various supports to reach the bell, to no avail. At last he tried jumping from the supports, but failed. The boy was exhausted and sat down on the ground in despair. A passerby, who had been watching from a bench across the street as this little boy tried hard to reach the bell, felt great pity for the boy. He stood up, crossed the street and rang the bell for him. Soon the gates opened and the boy was served food in the dharmashala.

After performing spiritual practices and doing whatever we can to purify ourselves, we have to simply wait patiently for the Master to bestow his grace on us. But we should be careful not to give up putting forth effort in the name of waiting for grace. Amma says, "It is all right if you faithfully wait for Him to come, but be sure you are attentive in your waiting. If you are preoccupied with other things, how can God come? How can His grace flow? It is foolishness to say, 'I am waiting for God, for His grace to come. He is all-com-passionate, so He will come. Until then, let me engage in other important matters.' You will neither receive grace nor will you have the power to overcome difficult situations with this kind of faith."

In the end, only grace can give us that knowledge of the Truth. But the only way to get that kind of grace is to ceaselessly put forth efforts toward the goal, just like the boy at the dharmashala was doing everything in his power to ring the bell. It was the boy's earnest efforts that attracted the man's attention and which moved his heart. Similarly when we strive earnestly to realize the Self, it will surely attract the Guru's grace, which will take us to the ultimate goal. For our part, we should strive wholeheartedly. Everything else will be looked after by the Master.

Chapter 19

Blessings in Disguise

In the last chapter, we defined grace as the factor that makes our efforts successful and helps us to accomplish our goals in life. It is true that grace sometimes works in this way, but it is not always so simple. As we continue along the spiritual path, we will find that perhaps even more than in success, it is in failure and hardship that grace is the most palpable. Perhaps it was with this in mind that the Greek playwright Aeschylus wrote, "He who learns must suffer. And even in our sleep, pain that cannot forget falls drop by drop upon the heart, and in our own despair, against our will, comes wisdom to us by the awful grace of God."

From 1985 onward, Amma started sending me out of the ashram to give satsang, meet with devotees and spend time at branch ashrams. From then on, the only extended period of time I would spend in Amma's presence would be during Her world tours. Now, Amma does the Japan-U.S. tour during the summer, comes back to Amritapuri for two months and then does Her European tour in October and November. But in those days, the Europe tour immediately followed the US tour, so I would be able to spend three continuous months in Amma's presence. This was always a blissful period for me, and I looked forward to it every year. But in 1989, something happened that made these tours very difficult for me. Whenever I went to Amma's room, She would find some reason to send me away. Either She would

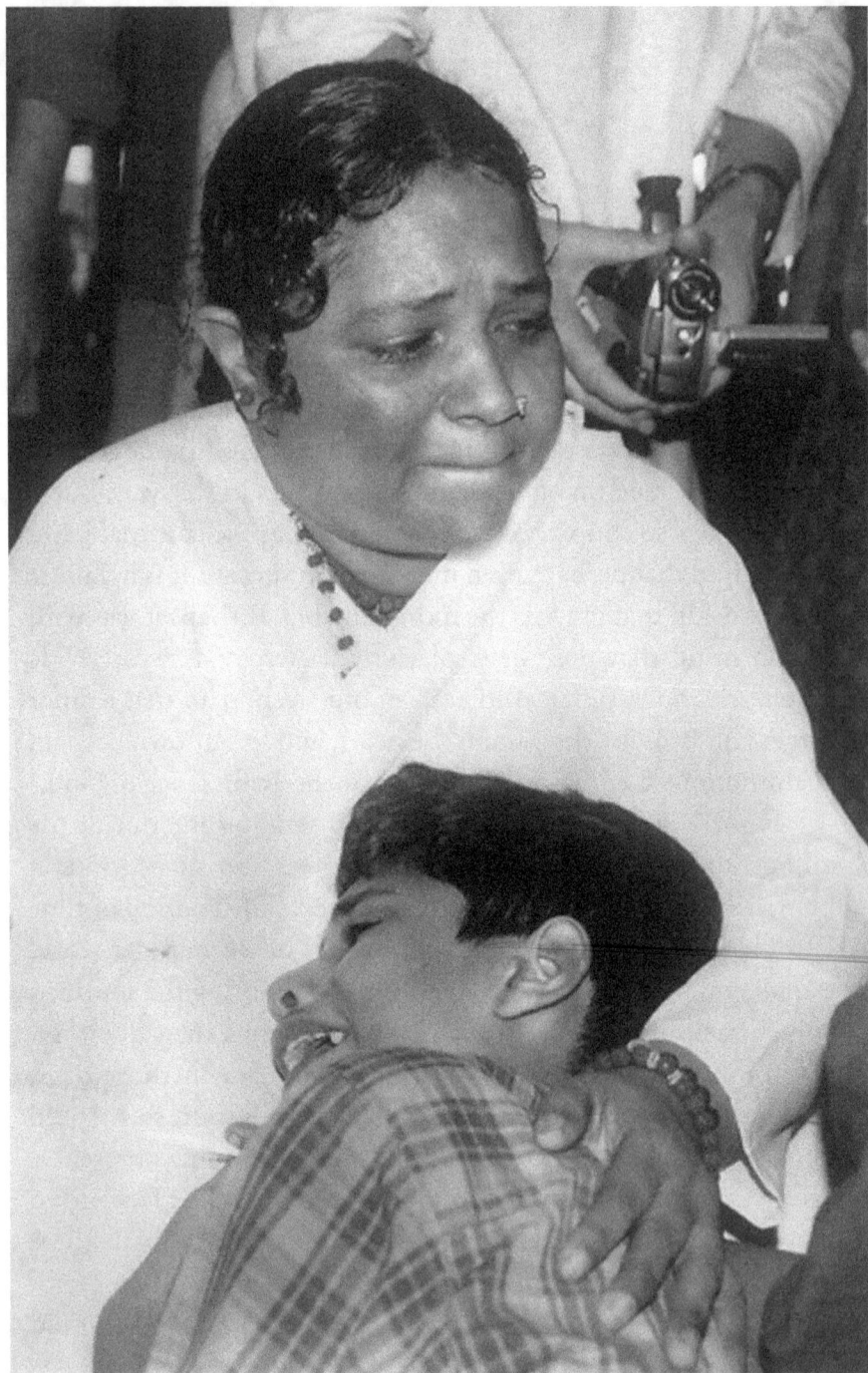

say that She was busy, or that She wanted to be left alone, or She would scold me for things which I had done improperly, and sometimes She would even blame me for things which I had not done. As time went on, I noticed that She was not doing this with any of the other swamis. When Amma treated me in this way, I felt very sad. But when I noticed that I was the only one She was treating this way, I felt even worse. I started making mistakes while playing the drum for Amma during the evening bhajans, and I was generally not at my best.

This treatment went on for the entire 1989 world tour, and throughout the 1990 world tour as well. Finally, some time during the 1990 world tour, Amma called me to Her room. I went to Her room hesitantly, wondering what was in store for me. I even thought that Amma might send me back to India, as I was not even playing the drum properly anymore.

When I entered Amma's room, Her mood was gentle. She patiently explained to me that I was going through a very bad period and that I was destined to undergo suffering and hardship at this time. That was why Amma had been treating me harshly. She also said that I should take some kind of vow in addition to my normal spiritual practices. She said that it was such a bad time for me that I might even leave the ashram.

Thinking about Amma's advice, I decided that since Amma was my all in all and I had no other God than Her, I would take a vow of silence and fasting on Thursdays, which is the day traditionally symbolic of worship of the Guru. I also realized that Amma's treatment of me had only been to help me exhaust my prarabdha without having to go through an even worse situation. According to the law of karma, I had to experience some kind of internal emotional suffering and anguish at that time. Amma helped me to go through that hardship without having to leave Her side.

Recently a young brahmachari who was serving as a *pujari* (temple priest) in one of Amma's Brahmasthanam temples came to Amma with tears in his eyes. When Amma asked him what was wrong, he explained that though most people in the area of the temple received him very warmly, there was one couple who were consistently cruel and abusive toward him. They even told him that his very presence disgusted them and if Amma did not send another brahmachari to replace him, they would stop coming to the temple. As he concluded his tale, he asked Amma plaintively, "Is my presence so disgusting, Amma?"

Amma wiped the boy's tears and consoled him, saying, "If anyone abuses you, don't pay any attention to their words." The brahmachari was comforted by Amma's words, but what She said next really surprised him. "Soon the day will come when hundreds of people will be vying for your attention!" His spirit renewed, the brahmachari returned to the Brahmasthanam Temple the next day. Amma's words had reassured him, even though he did not see how Her prediction could possibly come true.

Several months later, the day after the tsunami, Amma called this brahmachari and asked him to look after the physical and emotional needs of more than 700 children who had lost their homes and, in most cases, one or more family members as well. Over the following weeks and months, these children developed a deep-seated affection and respect for this brahmachari. Wherever he went he was followed by at least a dozen of these children, and seeing the success he had in inspiring, entertaining and disciplining them, the surviving relatives of these children began clamoring for his attention and advice as well.

Sometimes, according to our prarabdha, there is no way for us to avoid a painful experience; we have no choice but to endure it. The writer Chinua Achebe put it most eloquently: "When suffering knocks at your door and you say there is no seat for him, he tells you not to worry because he has brought his own stool." In such cases, however, Amma blesses us with the strength to face the situation with courage and equanimity.

Three years ago, I had to undergo two knee operations. Previously Amma had told me that it was a bad time for me, and that I should be careful about my health. Because Amma did not specifically say what kind of health problem I should watch out for, I didn't worry about it. I just surrendered the problem—whatever it might be—to Amma. One day, shortly thereafter, I began to feel severe pain in one of my knees. When I told Her about it, Amma asked me to go to the hospital immediately. After examining me, the doctors suggested that I undergo corrective surgery. Even though it was to be a minor operation, I was somewhat anxious because I had never before had any serious injury or ailment.

Amma told me that I should undergo the surgery, so I made plans to go ahead with the operation. I was in the United States at the time, and I would call Amma almost every day, praying to Her that She would somehow help me to avoid the surgery. Whenever I talked to Amma, She always reassured me, "Don't worry, my son. Everything will be okay."

From Amma's words, I was sure that the operation could be averted. However, when the day of the scheduled operation arrived, my condition had not improved. I had no choice but to have the surgery. The operation went smoothly, and afterward I called Amma. She said that even though I had been unable to see Her, She had been there with me during the surgery. Hearing Amma's words I felt very comforted. After the surgery, the pain went away.

Six months later, I had further problems in the same knee. The doctors informed me that a second surgery would be required. This time, Amma told me I should have the surgery at AIMS, Her super-specialty hospital in Cochin. The first time, I had been far away in the United States, and I wasn't able to see Amma for several days. If I had the surgery at AIMS, I would be able to see Amma within a couple of days, as AIMS is just three hours away from the ashram. I followed Amma's instructions and went ahead with the second operation. This time, knowing that Amma would be with me in subtle form during the operation and that I would be able to see Her soon after, I didn't feel any anxiety at all. Before then, I had been loathe to have even a shot in the arm, but after that experience, I don't feel any tension at all about any procedures I may have to undergo. In this case, Amma did not help me in the way I expected; She did not remove the problem. Instead, She gave me the courage to face the experience with equanimity.

True Masters rarely violate or interfere with the laws of the universe even though it is within their power to do so. They respect and abide by these laws, both because they have no special self-motivated desires to do otherwise and because from their level of consciousness they understand that these laws function only for the good of the world.

But there are examples of Mother Nature responding to the spontaneous *sankalpa*, or divine resolve, of Mahatmas like Amma. One year during Amma's programs in San Ramon, California, there was a terrible fire in the kitchen where they were preparing food for the hundreds of devotees who had come to see Amma. One of the brahmacharis who was with Amma on the veranda of Her house at the time later told me that at one point, Amma faced the fire and prayed with folded palms.

What took place afterward was truly amazing. The wind suddenly shifted directions and started blowing away from the tent and other ashram buildings. Of course some people were instantly hurt in the fire, but many more were saved from harm because the fire didn't spread.

Amma visited each of the injured devotees in the hospital and sat by their bedsides. Later, She explained that each of them had been destined to suffer much worse on that day or even lose their lives. By experiencing the accident at Amma's ashram, they were able to escape a worse fate.

Now almost all of them are back in the kitchen on Am-ma's US tour with even more enthusiasm and dedication than ever. They have all shared with me that they could feel Her presence and grace strongly throughout their difficulties, and that their faith in Amma has even deepened as a result of this experience. The fire injured their bodies but not their faith or their spirit. Without taking the accident in a negative way or dwelling on their fate, they have taken the accident as an opportunity to rededicate their lives at Amma's feet. They did not let it become a stumbling block in their lives but transformed it into a stepping-stone for spiritual growth instead.

Amma has said that the Guru removes 90 percent of our karma, leaving only the remaining 10 percent for us to undergo. But even then, we may wonder, "Why leave 10 percent? If the Guru can take 90 percent, why not 100 percent? What is so powerful or important about the law of karma that we must suffer at least 10 percent?" The answer is that this remaining 10 percent is what makes us grow and evolve spiritually.

Amma describes the attitude that a spiritual seeker should have in facing his or her karma: "A seeker is not worried whether fortune or misfortune befalls him. He knows that his karma is like an arrow that has already been released from the bow. Nothing can stop it. The arrow might hurt, injure or even kill him, but for him it doesn't matter. It is like the phonograph needle running in the grooves of a record. The song has to play as long as the needle of life goes through the grooves. The song may be a terrible one or a good one. Either way, he has produced it himself; it is his own voice. He will not want to run away from his karma because he knows that it is a process of purification and that it is cleansing the stains created by him in the past, in some previous life. And above all, the true seeker will always have the protection and grace of the Guru. Therefore, even in the most difficult times, he will receive solace and help."

Suffering comes as a shock to us only when it has been absent from our lives for a long time. We just have to ask the millions of people who live in abject poverty or in war-torn areas throughout the world. They will tell us how full of suffering life is. We just have to ask Amma. She knows better than anyone; millions of people around the world come to Her with countless problems, asking for Her grace and advice. Instead of questioning why we have to suffer, we should try to think of how fortunate we have been at other times in our life and be thankful to God that we were able to enjoy prosperity for so long.

Out of Her infinite compassion, Amma is giving Her guarantee that Her solace and help will be there in the most difficult times. Can we ask for anything more? I pray that we can all remember these words of Amma's whenever the hardships of life arise, and that She give us the right perception of these experiences so that they help us to grow and evolve on our spiritual path.

Chapter 20

Shower of Grace

A couple of months after the tsunami, Amma held two camps for the children who were affected by the disaster. During these camps, over 10,000 children stayed at the ashram participating in various classes on yoga, Sanskrit, and spoken English. Before coming to the ashram, many of the children could not even sleep through the night, so traumatized were they by the experience of the tsunami. Yet when they came to the ashram, even though they had never been there before or even met Amma, they seemed to forget all about their sorrows. Overnight, they became playful and joyful again, even quite naughty: they were changing the locks on people's doors; riding the elevator up and down making it stop at each and every floor; and one Western brahmachari who works in the residential buildings found himself wrestled to the ground by about a dozen eight-year-olds who wanted to test their strength.

Meanwhile, another Western devotee taught the children how to make paper airplanes. The next day there was an immediate need of a new position at the ashram: an air traffic controller. The children were throwing hundreds of paper airplanes from the 15th floor of the residential buildings.

Every day, Amma held a question-and-answer session with the children. Amma used the children's innocent questions as an opportunity to inculcate spiritual values in them. For example,

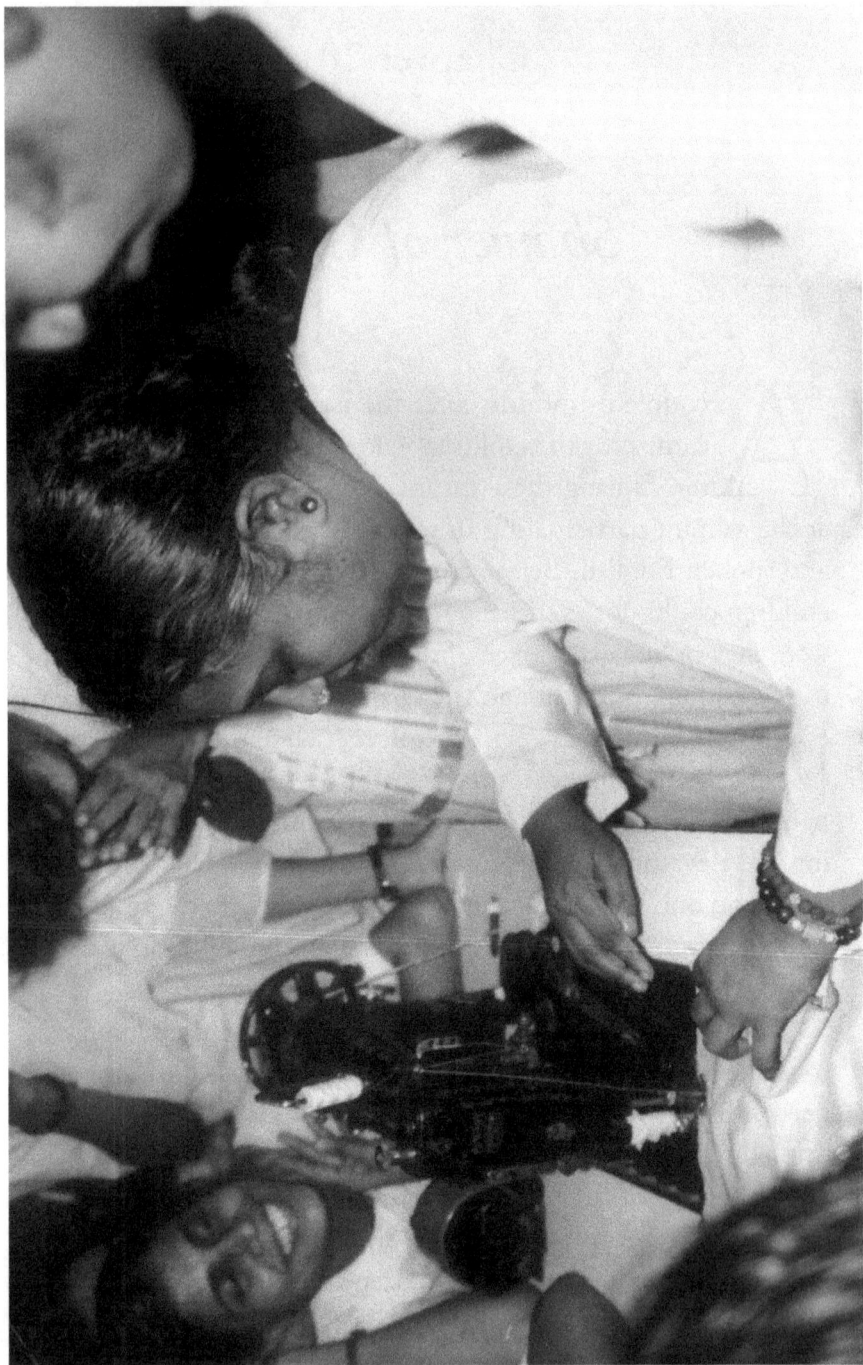

one afternoon one of the children told Amma that she had heard that idols in some temples over the years are slowly growing. "Is this possible?" the child wanted to know.

"God is a wonder," Amma said. "Anything is possible in God's creation. The idols may grow, but what about you? Have you grown? Have you changed? What is the point in looking at the change of the idol? It is you who have to change."

Another child asked Amma what Her real name was. "I also inquired into this," Amma said. "I don't have a name. People call me by different names."

Another child asked, "Amma, what is your mother's name?"

Amma's answer revealed once more the expansiveness of Her vision: "My foster mother's name is Damayanti,[3] but for me the earth is my mother, the sea is my mother, the sky is my mother, plants are my mother, the cow is my mother, animals are my mother. The very building in which we are sitting is also my mother."

Then a small girl came forward, "Amma, they say you have divine powers. Is it true?"

"What do you mean by divine powers?" Amma asked.

"That whatever Amma says will come true, that people who couldn't have children, they got children from you..."

"Ask the devotees," Amma said at first, not wanting to speak about Herself. "I prefer to be a small child, a beginner. Everybody wants to become the king of the village, and then they all fight. You have to become the king within." Amma added that the potential to accomplish such things is there in every one of us,

---

[3] Damayanti is the name of Amma's biological mother. By referring to her as a foster mother, Amma is pointing out that in each birth, we get a different, temporary mother, and our only permanent mother is God.

but that it is up to us to invoke it. The children cheered, greeting Amma's answer with applause.

The last day of the camp, one child stood up and asked, "Amma, what will happen to us when we leave here tomorrow?"

Amma asked him why he would ask such a question.

The boy replied, "Amma, the five days we spent here have completely changed our lives. Even though many of us lost a mother, a father, a sister or a brother in the tsunami, because of the love and attention you showered on us, we didn't feel the pain of losing them. Now we don't want to leave the ashram. We want to stay here forever."

Another child who participated in one of these camps told Amma during darshan, "Amma, in the tsunami we lost everything, but we found you. And do you know what? It was worth it."

After the camp was over, many of the local children could be seen frequenting the ashram on a regular basis; they now feel it is their own. Their parents and other adult villagers, who never used to set foot inside the ashram, now come for milk and groceries, medical care, clothing, counseling and even vocational training. The ashram has become an oasis of hope in what otherwise would have been a wasteland of despair, rendered barren and bleak by one of the worst natural disasters in the history of the world.

During Amma's 2004 world tour, Amma said that She saw dark clouds gathering on the horizon, and that we should all pray that these clouds be transformed into a shower of grace. In what has unfolded since, we can observe that while these dark clouds tormented so many lives in the form of the tsunami, they have also brought the shower of Amma's grace to so many people.

Amma says that when everything is going smoothly, when no one is suffering deeply, we will not be fully aware of the Master's compassionate nature. But when calamity strikes, the Master's compassion will manifest in its fullness. The greater the calamity, the more compassion will flow forth from the Master. Actually, the same degree of compassion is there at all times, but we are not able to perceive it. In fact, until the tsunami, I think none of us knew just how compassionate Amma truly is.

A minister of the Indian government who watched the footage of Amma's actions on the day of the tsunami commented on the fact that Amma's immediate reaction was to change Her clothes and wade down into the surging waters, urging everyone to go to higher levels where they would be safe. The minister said that if he had been in Amma's place, he would have first gone to a higher level and then asked everyone else to follow. But Amma did the opposite. In fact She insisted on being the very last person to leave the ashram that day. Even the ashram's elephants and cows had been evacuated to the mainland before Amma finally agreed to move to a safer location.

There were nearly 20,000 people in the ashram that day, and though the ashram was badly flooded, not a single person was hurt. Even the patients lying in beds at the ashram's charitable hospital were saved. Because Amma had relocated the darshan at the last minute to the old prayer hall that is one and a half stories above ground, there were no children playing in the large, ground-level open area that is the main darshan hall. Because Amma had rescheduled the pension distribution to take place on another day, 9,000 destitute women were spared from what would have been the brunt of the disaster as the water rushed into the large, open-air hall. When I think of this miraculous series of near-misses, I cannot help but be reminded of Lord Krishna holding up the Govardhana Mountain over the heads of the residents of his childhood home in order to protect them from a deluge. It was as if Amma literally picked up each and every person—and animal, for that matter—and held them above the rushing waters. Can this be called anything but divine grace?

Amma wouldn't leave the ashram until everyone else had, and then only because some of the disciples wouldn't go if She stayed behind. Finally Amma did cross the waters onto the mainland, sometime past midnight. It was clear She hadn't even drunk water all day, as Her lips were completely chapped. When one of the brahmacharis asked Her to drink something, Amma replied simply, "How can I take water when so many people have died?"

We are always ready to sit back and congratulate ourselves for doing one or two good things, saying to ourselves, "I have done my good deed for the day." But no matter how much Amma does for others, She never feels that it is enough.

Some years ago, there was a short period during which Amma wore a brace on Her wrist while She gave darshan. One day, She suddenly removed the brace and continued to give darshan without it. When one of the brahmacharis asked Her why She had done that, Amma replied, "When giving darshan, my hand should touch their body so they feel a connection with Amma and feel Her motherly affection. A plastic brace in between Amma's hand and their body will only obstruct this feeling." Amma is always ready to forget Her own suffering for the sake of others. In fact, She does not wear a brace anymore.

In *Viveka Chudamani*, Shankaracharya declares, "The Mahatmas have crossed the frightening ocean of birth and death. Without any reason or expectation, they help others also to cross over." Their compassion does not spring from a logical decision or one that benefits them in some way. They do this simply out of their infinite compassion for us. When Amma has been directly asked why She has dedicated Her life to wiping the tears of suffering humanity and uplifting them spiritually, She simply shrugs and says, "That is like asking the river why it flows or the sun why it shines. That is its nature. It cannot do otherwise."

Amma never feels that She has done enough for Her children. Even before the tsunami, Amma was working harder and longer hours than anyone has ever done in the history of the world, dedicated to the spiritual and material upliftment of as many people as possible—at times, it seems, all of humanity.

Even though most of the world has already forgotten about the tsunami and its victims, Amma says that Her mind is still filled with the sufferings and needs of the tsunami victims. Most people think that Amma goes back to Her room and lies down to rest after an arduous session of darshan. But the truth is that most of the time, She does not get any rest at all. During Her 2005 tour of the United States, six months after the disaster, one Devi Bhava darshan went from 6:30 p.m. until after noon the following day. And yet, when She was done, Amma went straight to Her room where She spent four hours talking on the phone to the residents of the ashram administering to Her tsunami relief efforts.

In the months after the disaster struck, some of the brahmacharis joked that even to get Amma's attention, one had to begin one's sentence with the word, "Tsunami." About Her dedication to this cause, Amma commented that She would not be satisfied until all of the tsunami victims whom She had taken under Her wing—in Kerala, Tamil Nadu, Pondicherry, Andaman & Nicobar Islands, and Sri Lanka—had their homes back and were able to get their lives back on track.

As of this writing, in August 2005, Amma's ashram is the only institution in India to have distributed new homes to the tsunami victims. The tsunami was a terrible tragedy indeed, and it shattered the lives and hopes of so many. But without Amma to take on their sorrows as Her own, these people would have had no light in their lives at all—no hope for a return to any kind of normal life. Thus one of the greatest natural disasters the world has ever seen brought forth the infinite compassion—and the infinite grace—of the greatest Mahatma the world has ever known.

There is a beautiful poem that describes the way divine grace can bless us in unexpected ways.

> *I asked God for strength that I might achieve,*
> *but I was made weak that I might learn to humbly obey God.*
>
> *I asked for health that I might do greater things,*
> *but I was given infirmity that I may do better things.*
>
> *I asked for riches that I might be happy,*
> *but I was given poverty that I might be wiser.*
>
> *I asked for power that I might have the praise of men,*
> *but I was given weakness that I might feel the need of God.*
>
> *I asked for all things that I might enjoy life,*
> *but I was given life that I might enjoy all things.*
>
> *I got nothing I asked for but everything I hoped for.*
> *Almost despite myself, my unspoken prayers were answered.*
>
> *I among all human beings am most richly blessed.*

There are always some blessings in our life—the question is whether or not we are able to recognize them as such. Amma says, "God is there, the Guru is there, and grace is always there. You have all the faculties to know and experience this. You have a map and have been given the directions in the form of the Guru's words. The wind of the Guru's grace is always blowing. The river of his divine being is always flowing, and the sun of his knowledge is always shining. He's done his part. His work was over long, long ago."

Now it is up to us to do our part. We are always standing under a shower of divine grace. Whether we open ourselves up to that grace and allow our hearts to blossom in divine love or close ourselves off and sink deeper into selfishness, delusion and despair is entirely up to us.

It is grace that allows us to meet a Master. It is grace that allows us to recognize a Master when we see one. And it is grace that the Master gives us. By Amma's grace, most of us are able to recognize at least a little of Her divinity and greatness. If we hold onto that divinity and make ourselves open—by performing good actions and cultivating a pure and innocent childlike heart—our life will certainly become more blessed and more peaceful and more rich. It cannot be otherwise. May Amma shower Her blessings on all of us.

Glossary

adharma – Unrighteousness. Deviation from natural harmony.

Advaita –Literally, "not two." Refers to non-dualism, the fundamental principle of Vedanta, the highest spiritual philosophy of Sanatana Dharma.

Amrita Kuteeram –Mata Amritanandamayi Math's housing project providing free homes for very poor families. Over 30,000 houses have so far been built and given away throughout India.

Amrita Vidyalayam – Primary schools established and administered by the Mata Amritanandamayi Math, dedicated to providing value-based education. At present there are over 50 Amrita Vidyalayam schools throughout India.

Amritapuri – The international headquarters of Mata Amritanandamayi Math, located at Amma's birthplace in Kerala, India.

Amritavarsham50 – Amma's 50th birthday celebration, held as an international dialogue-and-prayer event at Cochin, Kerala in September 2003, with the theme, "Embracing the World for Peace & Harmony." The four-day celebrations were attended by international entrepreneurs, peace-makers, educators, spiritual leaders, environmentalists, India's foremost political leaders and cultural artists, and more than 200,000 people per day, including representatives of each of the 191 member countries of the United Nations.

archana – Commonly refers to the chanting of the 108 or 1000 names of a particular deity (e.g. Lalita Sahasranama).

Arjuna – A great archer who is one of the heroes of the epic Mahabharata. It is Arjuna whom Krishna addresses in the Bhagavad Gita.

asana – Meditation rug.

asura – Demon.

Atman – The Self, or Consciousness.

AUM –(Also "Om.")According to the Vedic scriptures, this is the primordial sound in the universe and the seed of creation. All other sounds arise out of Om and resolve back into Om.

Avatar – Divine Incarnation. From Sanskrit root "ava–tarati" – "to come down."

avil – Flattened rice.

Bhagavad Gita – "Song of the Lord." The teachings Lord Krishna gave Arjuna at the beginning of the Mahabharata War. It is a practical guide for facing a crisis in our personal or social life and is the essence of Vedic wisdom.

bhajan – Devotional song.

bhakti – Devotion, service and love for the Lord.

bhava – Mood or attitude.

bhiksha – Alms

Bhishma –Patriarch of the Pandavas and Kauravas. Though he fought on the side of the Kauravas during the Mahabharata War, he was a champion of dharma and was sympathetic to the victorious Pandavas.

brahmachari – A celibate male disciple who practices spiritual disciplines under a master. (Brahmacharini is the female equivalent.)

brahmacharya – Celibacy, and control of the senses in general.

Brahman – The Ultimate Truth beyond any attributes. Also, the omniscient, omnipotent, omnipresent substratum of the universe.

Brahmasthanam Temple – Born out of Amma's divine intuition, these unique temples are open to everyone irrespective of their religion. The central icon is four–sided, displaying

Ganesha, Shiva, Devi and the Serpent, emphasizing the inherent unity underlying the manifold aspects of the Divine. At present, there are 17 such temples throughout India and one in Mauritius.

Brahmin – Priestly class of India.

damam – Restraint of the senses.

danam – Charity.

darshan – An audience with a holy person or a vision of the Divine.

daya – Compassion.

devas – Celestial beings.

Devi – Goddess. The Divine Mother.

Devi Bhava – "The Divine Mood of Devi." The state in which Amma reveals Her oneness and identity with the Divine Mother.

dharma – In Sanskrit, dharma means "that which upholds (creation)." Most commonly, it indicates the harmony of the universe. Other meanings include: righteousness, duty, responsibility.

Draupadi – Wife of the Pandavas.

Duryodhana – The eldest of the 100 Kaurava brothers. Usurped the throne to which Yudhishthira, eldest brother of the Pandavas, was the heir apparent. Through his hatred of the righteous Pandavas and his famous refusal to grant them even a blade of grass, Duryodhana made the Mahabharata War unavoidable.

gopi – The gopis were milkmaids who lived in Krishna's childhood home of Brindavan. They were Krishna's ardent devotees. They exemplify the most intense love for God.

gurukula – Literally, "Guru's clan." Traditional school where children live with a Guru who instructs them in scriptural and academic knowledge, while instilling spiritual values.

homa – Fire ceremony.

japa – Repetition of a mantra.

jiva, or **jivatman** – Individual soul. According to Advaita Vedanta, the jivatman is, in fact, not a limited individual soul, but one and the same as the Paramatman, or Brahman, the one Supreme Soul that constitutes both the material and intelligent cause of the universe.

jnana – Knowledge.

kaimanis – Hand cymbals.

karma – Conscious actions. Also, the chain of effects produced by our actions.

Kauravas – The 100 children of King Dhritharasthra and Queen Gandhari, of whom the unrighteous Duryodhana was the eldest. The Kauravas were the enemies of their cousins, the virtuous Pandavas, with whom they fought in the Mahabharata War.

Krishna – The principle incarnation of Vishnu. He was born into a royal family but grew up with foster parents and lived as a young cowherd in Brindavan where He was loved and worshipped by his devoted companions, the gopis and gopas. Krishna later established the city of Dwaraka. He was a friend and advisor to His cousins, the Pandavas, especially Arjuna, to whom He served as charioteer during the Mahabharata War, and to whom He revealed His teachings as the Bhagavad Gita.

Krishna Bhava – "The Divine Mood of Krishna." The state in which Amma revealed Her oneness and identity with Krishna. Initially, Amma used to give Krishna Bhava darshan immediately before giving Devi Bhava darshan. During Krishna

Bhava, She did not identify with the problems of the devotees who came for Her darshan but remained as a witness. Deciding that the people of the modern world primarily needed the love and compassion of God as the Divine Mother, Amma stopped giving Krishna Bhava darshan in 1985.

Kurukshetra – The battlefield where the Mahabharata War was fought.

Lalita Sahasranama – 1000 Names of the Divine Mother.

lila – Divine play.

lokah samastah sukhino bhavantu – Peace mantra meaning, "May all the beings in all the worlds be happy." Chanted daily by Amma's disciples and devotees all over the world for the peace and harmony of the whole world.

Mahabharata – One of the two great Indian historical epics, the other being the Ramayana. It is a great treatise on dharma. The story deals mainly with the conflict between the righteous Pandavas and the unrighteous Kauravas and the great war at Kurukshetra. Containing 100,000 verses, it is the longest epic poem in the world, written around 3,200 B.C. by the Sage Veda Vyasa.

Mahatma – Literally, "Great Soul." Though the term is now used more broadly, in this book Mahatma refers to one who abides in the Knowledge that he or she is one with the Universal Self, or Atman.

mala – Rosary.

mananam – Reflection. Second step of the three-step process to Self-realiza-tion outlined in Vedanta.

Mata Amritanandamayi Devi – Amma's official monastic name, meaning Mother of Immortal Bliss, often prefixed with Sri to denote auspiciousness.

maya – Illusion. According to Advaita Vedanta, it is maya that causes the jivatman to erroneously identify itself with the body, mind and intellect, instead of its true identity the Paramatman.

Meenakshi Devi – Form of the Divine Mother installed the famous Madurai temple.

nidhidhyasanam – Contemplation. Final step of the three-step process to Self-realization outlined in Vedanta.

nirguna – Without form.

pada puja – Ceremonial washing of the Guru's feet, or his or her sandals, as a demonstration of love and respect. Usually includes the pouring of pure water, yogurt, ghee, honey and rose water.

Pandavas – Five sons of King Pandu and the heroes of the epic Mahabharata.

payasam – Sweet pudding made with rice or noodles, cashews and milk.

prarabdha – The fruits of actions from previous lives that one is destined to experience in the present life.

prasad – Blessed offering or gift from a holy person or temple, often in the form of food.

puja – Ritualistic or ceremonial worship.

Rama – The divine hero of the epic Ramayana. An incarnation of Lord Vishnu, he is considered the ideal of dharma and virtue.

Ravana – Powerful demon. Vishnu incarnated as Lord Rama for the purpose of slaying Ravana and thereby restoring harmony to the world.

Rishis – Self–realized Seers or Sages who perceive the mantras.

sadhana – Spiritual practice.

saguna – With form.

sakshi bhava – The attitude of remaining a witness to the body, mind and intellect.

samadhi – Oneness with God. A transcendental state in which one loses all sense of individual identity.

samsara – The cycle of birth and death.

Sanatana Dharma – "The Eternal Way of Life." The original and traditional name for Hinduism.

sankalpa – Divine resolve.

sannyasin – A monk who has taken formal vows of renunciation (sannyasa). A sannyasin traditionally wears an ochre–colored cloth representing the burning away of all desires. The female equivalent is a sannyasini.

Satguru – Literally, "True Master." All Satgurus are Mahatmas, but not all Mahatmas are Satgurus. The Satguru is one who, while still experiencing the bliss of the Self, chooses to come down to the level of ordinary people in order to help them grow spiritually.

satsang – Being in communion with the Supreme Truth. Also being in the company of the Mahatmas, listening to a spiritual talk or discussion, and participating in spiritual practices in a group setting.

seva – Selfless service, the results of which are dedicated to God.

Shankaracharya – Mahatma who re-established, through his works, the supremacy of the Advaita philosophy of non-duality at a time when Sanatana Dharma was on the decline.

Shiva – Worshipped as the first and foremost in the lineage of Gurus, and as the formless substratum of the universe in relationship to the creatrix Shakti. He is the Lord of destruction (of ego) in the trinity of Brahma (Lord of creation), Vishnu (Lord of preservation), and Shiva. Usually depicted as a monk, with ash all over his body, snakes in his hair, wearing only a loincloth and with a begging bowl and a trident in his hands.

shruti – "That which came down through hearing." Refers to the scriptures of Sanatana Dharma, which until recently were passed down through an oral tradition.

Sita – Rama's holy consort. In India, she is considered to be the ideal of womanhood.

sravanam – Listening. First step of the three-step process to Self-realization outlined in Vedanta.

Srimad Bhagavatam – Devotional text detailing the various incarnations of Lord Vishnu, with special emphasis on the Life of Sri Krishna. Written by the Sage Veda Vyasa after he completed the Mahabharata.

Sudhamani – Amma's name, given by her parents at the time of birth, meaning "Ambrosial Jewel."

tapas – Austerities, penance.

Upanishad – The portions of the Vedas dealing with the philosophy of non-dualism.

vairagya –Detachment. Especially detachment from all that is impermanent, i.e. the entire visible world.

vasana – Latent tendencies or subtle desires within the mind which manifest as action and habits.

Vedanta – "The end of the Vedas." It refers to the Upanishads, which deal with the subject of Brahman, the Supreme Truth, and the path to realize that Truth.

Vedantin – Practitioner of the philosophy of Vedanta.

Vedas – Most ancient of all scriptures, the Vedas were not composed by any human author but were "revealed" in deep meditation to the ancient Rishis. The mantras composing the Vedas are always there in nature in the form of subtle vibrations; the Rishis attained such a deep state of absorption that they were able to perceive these mantras.

vishwarupa – Cosmic form.

viveka – Discrimination. Especially discrimination between the Permanent and the impermanent.

Viveka Chudamani – Crest-Jewel of Discrimination. An introductory text on Vedanta, authored by Adi Shankaracharya. Recommended to be studied before studying the Upanishads.

yagna – Sacrifice, in the sense of offering something in worship or performing an action for personal as well as communal benefits.

yoga – "To unite." Union with the Supreme Being. A broad term, it also refers to the various practical methods through which one can attain oneness with the Divine. A path that leads to Self-realization.

yogi – A practitioner or an adept of yoga.

Yudhishthira – Eldest of the five Pandavas, and the rightful heir to the Kuru throne which had been usurped by the evil-minded prince Duryodhana. Said to have been the incarnation of the principle of dharma in a human form.